The Italian
Country Table

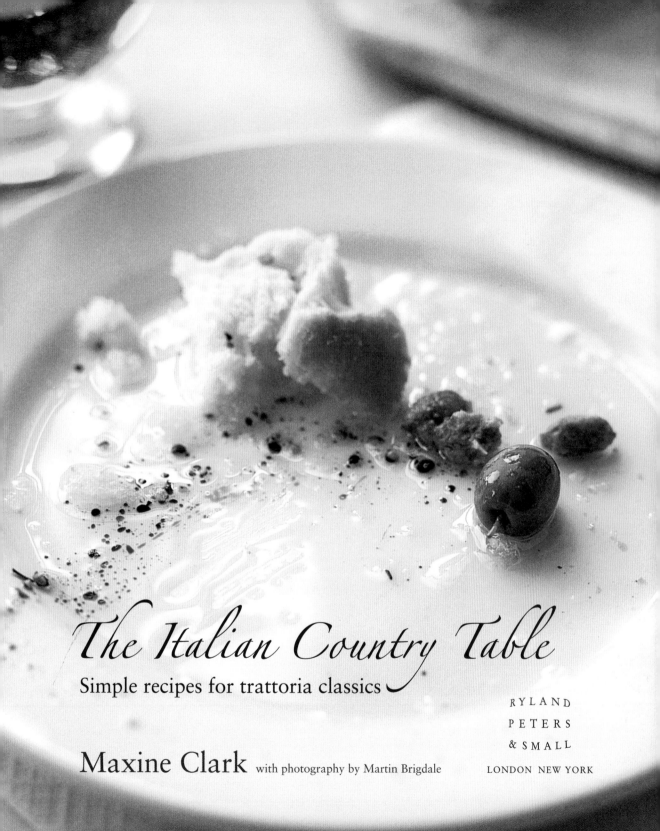

The Italian Country Table

Simple recipes for trattoria classics

Maxine Clark with photography by Martin Brigdale

RYLAND
PETERS
& SMALL

LONDON NEW YORK

DESIGN AND PHOTOGRAPHIC ART
DIRECTION Steve Painter
SENIOR COMMISSIONING EDITOR
Julia Charles
PRODUCTION Toby Marshall
ART DIRECTOR
Leslie Harrington
PUBLISHING DIRECTOR
Alison Starling

FOOD STYLISTS Maxine Clark
and Linda Tubby
PROP STYLISTS Helen Trent
and Róisín Nield
INDEXER Hilary Bird

First published in 2011
by Ryland Peters & Small
20–21 Jockey's Fields
London WC1R 4BW
and
Ryland Peters & Small, Inc.
519 Broadway, 5th Floor
New York NY10012
www.rylandpeters.com

10 9 8 7 6 5 4 3 2 1

Printed in China

Text © Maxine Clark 2004, 2006,
2007, 2011
Design and photographs © Ryland
Peters & Small 2011

ISBN: 978 1 84975 157 5

A CIP record for this book is
available from the British Library.

US Library of congress cataloging-
in-publication data has been
applied for.

The recipes in this book have been
published previously by Ryland
Peters & Small in *Trattoria* and
Flavours of Tuscany.

NOTES

- All spoon measurements are level, unless otherwise specified.
- All eggs are medium, unless otherwise specified. It is generally recommended that free-range eggs be used. Uncooked or partially cooked eggs should not be served to the very young, the very old, those with compromised immune systems, or to women who are pregnant.
- When a recipe calls for the grated zest/peel of citrus fruit, buy unwaxed fruit and wash well before using. If you can find only treated fruit, scrub well in warm soapy water and rinse before using.
- Ovens should be preheated to the specified temperature. Recipes in this book were tested using a regular oven. If using a fan-assisted oven, follow the manufacturer's instructions for adjusting your oven's temperatures

Contents

Introduction

A trattoria is a small restaurant, often family-run, producing homely meals from good, fresh, local ingredients. The menu will be short, change seasonally, but will not be adventurous – for the soul of trattoria food lies in tried and trusted recipes passed down through generations, often evoking memories of meals eaten at home cooked by your mother or grandmother during childhood. You feel safe in a cosy, welcoming trattoria. The bustling family atmosphere, still key to Italian life, and the familiar smells assailing your nostrils will cocoon you like a security blanket.

Successful trattorias can stay in the same family for generations – the job of cooking passing from grandfather or grandmother to daughter or son and so on. Gender does not matter in the kitchen: it's the ability to cook with love that matters. When grandparents become too frail to stand the rigours of a busy kitchen, they fulfil other useful jobs such as prepping vegetables, giving advice (wanted or not!), waiting at tables, manning the cash desk, or taking time to make one dish that remains their personal speciality. After service has finished at lunch or dinner, the family will sit around a table and eat their own meal, discussing family matters and the events of the day. Locality, good food and a warm welcome are the traditional hallmarks.

I have been fortunate enough to cook, eat, teach, wash up, sing, make friends, share jokes, cry and play in some wonderful Italian kitchens. In all of them I have learned, and am still learning, cooking techniques, Italian kitchen lore and some very useful Italian words and phrases. All the Italian cooks I have worked with over the years have willingly shared with me their bountiful knowledge which I, in turn, now wish to share with you in these regional recipes gathered during my travels in Italy.

Italian cooking techniques are simple, because good natural ingredients need nothing much done to them to create great food. Cook with care and attention to the recipe, the taste and texture of the dish. Taste, taste, taste – if you don't taste a dish from beginning to end, you can't monitor the changes that take place during cooking. Start using your nose too and you will identify how to tell if a dish is ready just by smell alone. But, above all, don't be scared of using your hands – you have to feel food to understand it – and hands were there long before spoons! Have confidence in yourself and your cooking and this will show in the finished dish – much of the joy of cooking is in the preparation and in the reward of a dish that you have created yourself – no matter how simple.

With the best quality ingredients, a little basic cooking knowledge and a big warm cook's heart, you are ready to cook Italian food at home.

Appetizers

The combination of sweet, salty Parma ham or a local prosciutto crudo and a yielding soft fruit like ripe figs or melon is one of life's little miracles. This is an all-time classic, and none the worse for that. I have been served this with a drizzle of aged balsamic vinegar over the figs, which was amazing. If you find a really aged balsamic vinegar on your travels, buy it – never mind the expense. It will be thick, sweet and syrupy, and heaven to use in tiny amounts. In another tiny trattoria I visited, prosciutto was wrapped around halved figs that were then brushed with olive oil and lightly grilled over hot charcoal. This is quick to assemble, providing you have excellent, thinly sliced ham and perfect, garnet-centred figs.

Parma ham with figs and balsamic dressing

Prosciutto di Parma con fichi e balsamico

4 large or 8 small fresh ripe figs (preferably purple ones)

1 tablespoon good quality aged balsamic vinegar

extra virgin olive oil

12 thin slices of Italian dry-cured ham, such as *prosciutto di Parma* or *proscuitto crudo*

150 g/5½ oz. fresh Parmesan, broken into craggy lumps

To serve

extra virgin olive oil

crushed black pepper

Serves 4

Take each fig and stand it upright. Using a sharp knife, make 2 cuts across each fig not quite quartering it, but keeping it intact. Ease the figs open and brush with balsamic vinegar and olive oil.

Arrange 3 slices of Parma ham on each plate with the figs and Parmesan on top. Sprinkle with extra virgin olive oil and plenty of crushed black pepper.

Fresh beans with pecorino and prosciutto

Baccelli con pecorino e prosciutto crudo

One of the simplest appetizers in Tuscany is a pile of freshly podded young broad/fava beans served with young pecorino and locally cured prosciutto crudo. As simple as that. These springtime beans are called baccelli, and are eaten in the Livorno area with a type of lightly salted pecorino-type cheese known as bacellone. Another younger, fresh local cheese is marzolino, equally delicious. The contrast of fresh green beans, creamy, salty cheese and fruity, salty meat is divine. Tuscans eat the beans skins and all, but this is recommended only when the beans are very young.

500 g/1 lb. fresh young unshelled broad/fava beans, or 175 g/ 6 oz. frozen beans, thawed

115 g/4 oz. young pecorino, preferably not the hard grating kind

6 slices Italian dry-cured ham, such as *prosciutto crudo*

5 tablespoons olive oil

freshly squeezed juice of ½ a lemon

2 teaspoons chopped fresh oregano

2 tablespoons chopped fresh flat-leaf parsley

a pinch of dried chilli/hot pepper flakes (optional)

sea salt and freshly ground black pepper

Serves 4

Remove the beans from their shells, blanch in boiling water for 20 seconds, drain and refresh, then pop them out of their skins and place in a bowl. If using frozen beans, thaw then pop them out of their skins and put in a bowl.

Cut the pecorino into cubes and cut the ham into strips, then add to the beans. Whisk together the olive oil, lemon juice, oregano, parsley and dried chilli/hot pepper flakes, if using, and pour over the bean mixture. Toss together and season to taste with salt and pepper. Serve immediately.

Baked mussels with crispy breadcrumbs

Cozze gratinate

The contrast of the golden crunchy breadcrumbs and the soft mussel meat is fantastic. Although this recipe may seem a lot of work, it is well worth it. Mussels are known as cozze in Italian, but called muscoli in Tuscany.

1.5 kg/3 lbs. live mussels, cleaned (see Note)

150 ml/scant ⅔ cup white wine

2 garlic cloves, lightly crushed

3 tablespoons olive oil, plus extra for drizzling

1 onion, very finely chopped

150 g/¼ cup stale (but not dried) breadcrumbs

4 tablespoons finely chopped fresh flat-leaf parsley

freshly squeezed juice of 1 lemon

sea salt and freshly ground black pepper

a large baking dish or 4 individual baking dishes

Serves 4

Put the mussels in a large saucepan, add the wine and garlic, cover tightly with a lid and cook over high heat for 4–5 minutes until they JUST start to open. Discard any that do not open. Strain through a colander and reserve the juices.

When the mussels have cooled, twist off all the empty shells and arrange the mussels in a single layer in a large baking dish or individual baking dishes set on a baking sheet.

Preheat the oven to 220°C (425°F) Gas 7. Heat the olive oil in a frying pan/skillet, add the onion and sauté for about 5 minutes, until soft. Reduce the heat, add the breadcrumbs and parsley and stir so that all the breadcrumbs absorb the oil. Cook for 5 minutes to brown the breadcrumbs a little.

Sprinkle this mixture over the mussels, drizzle over the extra olive oil and the lemon juice and bake in the preheated oven for 5 minutes. Reheat the strained liquid in a saucepan, add salt and pepper to taste (take care not to over season because the liquid may already be salty), then pour it around the mussels before serving.

NOTE: To prepare mussels, put them in a bowl of cold water and rinse several times to remove any grit or sand. Then scrub and debeard them. Tap all the mussels against the work surface. Discard any that don't close – they are dead – and also any with damaged shells. Keep them in a bowl of cold water until ready to cook.

One of the finest sights in a southern Italian fish market is a whole tuna fish being deftly portioned by men wielding the sharpest of cleavers, singing and shouting to come and buy their magnificent catch. You can be sure it is spanking fresh, and it is perfect for making carpaccio – the Italian equivalent of sashimi. Chilling or lightly freezing it makes it firm enough to slice very thinly. As soon as the slices hit plates at room temperature, they become meltingly soft. I have also seen smoked salmon and smoked swordfish served this way.

Fresh tuna carpaccio Carpaccio di tonno

250 g/9 oz. piece of sashimi-grade tuna or swordfish or swordfish loin (thin end)

125 g/5 oz. rocket/arugula

freshly shaved Parmesan, to serve

Dressing

freshly squeezed juice of 3 lemons

150 ml/⅔ cup extra virgin olive oil

1 garlic clove, finely chopped

1 tablespoon salted capers, rinsed and chopped

a pinch of dried chilli/hot pepper flakes

sea salt and freshly ground black pepper

Serves 4

Trim the tuna of any membrane or gristle. Wrap it tightly in clingfilm/plastic wrap and freeze for about 1 hour, until just frozen but not rock solid.

Meanwhile, to make the dressing, put the lemon juice, olive oil, garlic, capers, dried chilli/hot pepper flakes, salt and pepper in a bowl and whisk until emulsified.

Unwrap the tuna, slice it very thinly with a sharp, thin-bladed knife. Arrange the slices so they completely cover 4 large plates. Spoon the dressing over the top. Add a tangle of rocket/arugula and sprinkle with Parmesan shavings to serve.

There's nothing quite like these light, fresh, silvery morsels eaten fillet by fillet with a glass of chilled vino bianco, while you are overlooking a peacock sea with a warm salty breeze on your face. If you've never tried a fresh anchovy before, and see them in a market – buy them. They are mild and fresh, and the combination of lemon, parsley and olive oil is lifted by the zing of spring onions/scallions. Anchovies like these are found all over coastal areas, but you can make this dish with any small fish such as tiny sardines or even sprats.

Marinated fresh anchovies Acciughe al limone

16 fresh anchovies, small sardines or sprats

freshly squeezed juice of 2 lemons

2 fat spring onions/scallions, thinly sliced

2 tablespoons chopped fresh flat-leaf parsley

extra virgin olive oil

sea salt and freshly ground black pepper

crusty bread, to serve

Serves 4

To clean the anchovies, cut off the heads and slit open the bellies. Remove the insides (there isn't very much there at all) under running water. Slide your thumb along the backbone to release the flesh along its length. Take hold of the backbone at the head end and lift it out. The fish should now open up like a book. At this stage you can decide whether to cut it into 2 long fillets or leave whole – size will dictate. Pat them dry with paper towels.

Pour the lemon juice through a strainer into a shallow non-reactive dish and add the anchovies in an even layer, skin side up. Cover and let marinate in the refrigerator for 24 hours.

The next day, lift them out of the lemon juice – they will look pale and cooked. Arrange them on a serving dish and sprinkle with the spring onions/scallions, parsley and a large quantity of olive oil, season with salt and pepper and serve at room temperature with crusty bread.

Three marinated antipasti

Melanzane con salame e carciofi
Zucchine alla griglia marinate al limone
Involtini di peperoni

Melanzane

1 aubergine/eggplant, about 200 g/7 oz.

6 tablespoons olive oil, plus extra for brushing

8 thin slices salami

4 artichokes marinated in oil, drained and halved

freshly squeezed juice of ½ a lemon

1 tablespoon salted capers, rinsed and chopped

sea salt and freshly ground black pepper

Zucchine

3 courgettes/zucchini

4 tablespoons olive oil, plus extra for brushing

freshly squeezed juice of ½ a lemon

1 tablespoon freshly grated Parmesan

2 anchovies, rinsed and finely chopped

Involtini

2 large red (bell) peppers

150 g/5½ oz. fresh mozzarella

8 large fresh basil leaves

1 tablespoon good quality fresh green pesto

extra virgin olive oil

sea salt and freshly ground black pepper

toothpicks

Serves 4

All too often, antipasti can be very dull, but with a little imagination, you can work wonders with the simplest of ingredients. Marinating these morsels first gives them extra savour. The best antipasti are an appealing mix of colours, flavours and textures, to whet the palate ready for the meal ahead so do serve all three of these dishes together.

TO MAKE THE MELANZANE, heat a ridged stovetop grill pan/griddle until hot. Cut the aubergine/eggplant into 8 thin slices, brush lightly with olive oil and cook for 2–3 minutes on each side. Put a slice of salami on each one, then a halved artichoke at one side. Fold the aubergine/eggplant in half to cover the artichoke, secure with a toothpick and put in a shallow dish. Put the 6 tablespoons olive oil in a bowl, whisk in the lemon juice, capers, salt and pepper, then spoon over the aubergines/eggplants. Cover and let marinate for at least 2 hours.

TO MAKE THE ZUCCHINE, cut the courgettes/zucchini into long thin slices, brush with olive oil and cook on the same ridged stovetop grill pan/griddle for 2–3 minutes on each side. Transfer to a shallow dish. Put the olive oil, lemon juice, Parmesan and anchovies in a bowl, beat with a fork, then pour over the courgettes/zucchini. Cover and let marinate for at least 2 hours.

TO MAKE THE INVOLTINI, chargrill the peppers until soft and black. You can do this by piercing them with a fork and holding over a gas flame, or under a preheated grill/broiler. Rinse off the charred skin, cut the peppers into quarters lengthwise, cut off the stalks and scrape out the seeds. Cut the mozzarella into 8 thin slices. Put a slice inside each pepper strip, put a basil leaf on top and season well with salt and pepper. Roll up from one end and secure with a toothpick. Put the pesto in a bowl and beat in enough olive oil to thin it to pouring consistency. Add the pepper rolls and toss to coat. Cover and let marinate for at least 2 hours.

Caponata is rather like ratatouille, but much more exotic. There are dozens of variations of this delectable dish from Sicily, and it is a stalwart on the trattoria menu. Its origins are in little coastal bars (caupone in Sicilian) frequented by fishermen in the old days. It often contained soaked, dried ship's biscuit to pad it out and satisfy voracious appetites after a long fishing trip. The biscuit has long since disappeared and the dish has become somewhat refined. It improves with age, so I like to make a big batch and keep in the refrigerator or preserve in large jars. It's served as an antipasto, but is delicious with grilled fish or steak. As always in Sicily and in hot weather, serve at room temperature – it tastes much better.

Sweet and sour sicilian aubergine stew Caponata

4 aubergines/eggplants, cut into bite-size cubes

4 tablespoons extra virgin olive oil

1 onion, chopped

2 celery stalks/ribs, sliced

12 large ripe tomatoes, coarsely chopped, or 1½ x 400-g/14-oz. cans chopped tomatoes

1–2 tablespoons salted capers, rinsed well

100 g/½ cup pitted green olives

2 tablespoons red wine vinegar

2 teaspoons sugar

vegetable oil, for frying

sea salt

To serve

200 g/7 oz. fresh ricotta

toasted chopped almonds

chopped fresh flat-leaf parsley

an electric deep-fryer (optional)

Serves 6

Put the aubergines/eggplants in a colander, sprinkle with salt and let drain for 30 minutes.

Heat the olive oil in a saucepan and add the onion and celery. Cook for 5 minutes until softened but not browned. Add the tomatoes and cook for 15 minutes until pulpy. Add the capers, olives, vinegar and sugar to the sauce and cook for a further 15 minutes.

Rinse the aubergine/eggplant cubes and pat them dry with paper towels.

Heat sufficient vegetable oil in a deep-fryer to 190°C (375°F). Add the aubergine/eggplant cubes in batches and fry until deep golden brown. (This may take some time, but cook them thoroughly because undercooked aubergine/eggplant is unpleasant.) Alternatively, toss the cubes in olive oil, spread out in a roasting pan and roast in an oven preheated to 200°C (400°F) Gas 6 for 20 minutes, until well browned and tender. Drain well.

Stir the aubergines/eggplants into the sauce. Taste and adjust the seasoning (this means adding more sugar or vinegar to taste, to balance the flavours). Set aside for at least 30 minutes or overnight to develop the flavours before serving. Serve warm or at room temperature, spooned into shallow serving bowls and topped with the ricotta, almonds and parsley.

Asparagus with egg and truffle butter

Asparagi al burro d'oro

During the season, asparagus in all its varieties – from purple-tipped, to green, or white (the beloved one) – is often served with egg in some form, especially in the north of Italy. I have eaten this in spring in the lovely town of Asolo. All trattorie will have fresh asparagus on the menu at this time, and it is eaten as if it will never appear again. To our taste, asparagus is overcooked in Italy, especially in restaurants, but this is how they serve it, and I must say, the slightly longer cooking does bring out the flavour. The truffle oil is an optional luxury – you could add some chopped tarragon to the butter instead if preferred – but, it is wonderful with egg and asparagus.

4 very fresh eggs
90 g/6 tablespoons softened
 unsalted butter
a little truffle oil (optional)
500 g/1 lb. fresh asparagus
sea salt and freshly ground
 black pepper

Serves 4

Hard-boil the eggs for about 10 minutes, depending on their size. Cool in cold water, then peel. Halve the eggs and remove the yolks. Finely chop the whites and reserve. Mash the yolks with the butter until well blended. Add a drop or two of truffle oil, if using, and season with salt. Cover and keep at room temperature.

Trim the asparagus. Steam for about 12 minutes, until tender. Arrange on 4 warmed serving plates, sprinkle with chopped egg white, salt and pepper, then serve with the golden butter. (The butter can be either spooned on top to melt into the spears or served in little dishes to spread onto each mouthful.)

Soups

Pappa al pomodoro is only as good as its ingredients – great tomatoes, good bread and wonderful, green olive oil. This is one of the most comforting soups on earth and of course has its origins in peasant thrift. Leftover bread is never thrown away in Tuscany – there is always a use for it. Here, it thickens a rich tomato soup, which is in turn enriched with Parmesan (a nod to modern tastes, because an aged local pecorino would have been used instead). You see this soup on every menu around Florence, Siena and Arezzo. My own addition is the basil oil – in Tuscany you would be given locally produced olive oil at the table to pour over the soup yourself.

Creamy tomato and bread soup with basil oil

Pappa al pomodoro con olio verde

1.5 litres/6 cups good quality
  vegetable stock

4 tablespoons olive oil

1 onion, chopped

1.25 kg/2 lbs. 12 oz. very ripe, soft
  tomatoes, coarsely chopped

300 g/10 oz. stale white bread,
  thinly sliced, crusts removed

3 garlic cloves, crushed

125 g/1 cup freshly grated
  Parmesan, plus extra to serve

sea salt and freshly ground
  black pepper

Basil oil

6 tablespoons chopped fresh basil

150 ml/⅔ cup extra virgin olive oil

Serves 6

Heat the stock slowly in a large saucepan.

Meanwhile, heat the oil in a second large saucepan, add the onion and tomatoes and sauté over gentle heat for about 10 minutes, until soft. Push the mixture through a food mill, mouli or sieve/strainer, and stir into the hot stock. Add the bread and garlic.

Cover and simmer gently for about 45 minutes, until thick and creamy, whisking from time to time to break up the bread. Take care, because this soup can catch on the bottom on the pan.

To make the basil oil, put the basil and olive oil in a blender and blend until completely smooth – if not, pour through a fine sieve/strainer.

To finish, stir the Parmesan into the soup, then add salt and pepper to taste. Ladle into warmed serving bowls and drizzle 2 tablespoons basil oil over each one. Serve hot, warm or cold (but not chilled), with more Parmesan on the side for sprinkling.

Bean and vegetable soup with cabbage La ribollita

There's nothing quite like a huge bowl of thick, warming soup on a damp evening beside a crackling, scented log fire. Best made in large quantities, this is a great recipe for a family get-together and is very filling. Ribollita means 'reboiled', and is made from whatever vegetables are around, but must contain beans and the delicious Tuscan black winter cabbage, cavolo nero. I know I am back in Tuscany when I see it growing in rows in small allotments, looking like mini palm trees. Savoy cabbage makes a good alternative. The basic bean and vegetable soup is made the day before, then reheated and ladled over toasted garlic bread, drizzled with olive oil and served with Parmesan.

250 g/1½ cups dried cannellini beans or other white beans

150 ml/⅔ cup extra virgin olive oil

1 onion, finely chopped

1 carrot, chopped

1 celery stalk/rib, chopped

2 leeks, finely chopped

4 garlic cloves, finely chopped, plus 1 extra peeled and bruised, for rubbing

1 small white cabbage, finely sliced

1 large potato, chopped

4 courgettes/zucchini, chopped

400 ml/1¾ cups passata (Italian strained tomatoes)

2 sprigs of fresh rosemary

2 sprigs of fresh thyme

2 sprigs of fresh sage

1 dried red chilli/hot pepper

500 g/1 lb. cavolo nero (Tuscan black cabbage) or Savoy cabbage, finely sliced

6 thick slices of crusty white bread

sea salt and freshly ground black pepper

To serve

extra virgin olive oil

freshly grated Parmesan

Serves 8

Put the beans in a bowl, cover with cold water, soak overnight, then drain just before you're ready to use them.

Next day, heat half the olive oil in a large, heavy saucepan or stockpot and add the onion, carrot and celery. Cook gently for 10 minutes, stirring frequently. Add the leeks and garlic and cook for 10 minutes. Add the white cabbage, potato and courgettes/zucchini, stir well and cook for 10 minutes, stirring frequently.

Stir in the soaked beans, passata, rosemary, thyme, sage, dried chilli/hot pepper, salt and plenty of pepper. Cover with about 2 litres/8 cups water (the vegetables should be well covered), bring to the boil, then turn down the heat and simmer, covered, for at least 2 hours, until the beans are very soft.

Take out 2–3 large ladlefuls of soup and mash well. Stir back into the soup to thicken it. Stir in the cavolo nero or Savoy cabbage and simmer for another 15 minutes.

Remove from the heat, let cool, then refrigerate overnight. The next day, slowly reheat the soup and stir in the remaining olive oil. Toast the bread and rub with the extra garlic clove. Pile the bread into warmed soup bowls and ladle the soup over the top. Drizzle in more olive oil and serve immediately with plenty of freshly grated Parmesan.

Tuscan bean soup with rosemary

Zuppa di toscanelli al rosmarino

This is a simple soup that can be found in various guises all over central and northern Italy. To give it a sophisticated touch, I sauté sliced garlic, rosemary and chilli in really good olive oil, just enough to release their aromas, and spoon this over the soup just before serving. The aroma is intoxicating. Like many other rugged soups, it is often served as a meal in itself ladled over toasted country bread.

250 g/1½ cups dried white or brown beans (such as haricot, borlotti or cannellini)

a pinch of bicarbonate of soda/baking soda

cold water, or good quality chicken or vegetable stock (see method)

a handful of fresh sage leaves, plus 2 tablespoons finely chopped fresh sage

4 garlic cloves

300 ml/scant 1¼ cups olive oil

2 tablespoons chopped fresh rosemary needles

a large pinch of dried chilli/hot pepper flakes

sea salt and freshly ground black pepper

coarsely chopped fresh flat-leaf parsley, to serve

Serves 6

Put the beans in a bowl, cover with cold water, add the bicarbonate of soda/baking soda and leave to soak overnight.

Preheat the oven to 160°C (325°F) Gas 3. Drain the beans and put them in a flameproof casserole dish. Cover with cold water or chicken or vegetable stock to a depth of 5 cm/2 inches above the beans, and push in the sage leaves. Bring to the boil, cover tightly with a lid and transfer to the preheated oven for about 1 hour, until tender. (The time depends on the freshness of the beans so test after 40 minutes.) Keep them in their cooking liquid.

Meanwhile, finely chop 2 of the garlic cloves and thinly slice the other 2. Put half the beans, the cooked sage and all the liquid into a blender or food processor and blend until smooth. Pour back into the remaining beans in the casserole dish. Add a little extra water or stock to thin the soup if necessary.

Heat half the olive oil in a frying pan/skillet and add the chopped garlic. Sauté gently until soft and golden, then add the chopped sage and cook for 30 seconds. Stir this into the soup and reheat until boiling. Simmer gently for 10 minutes. Add salt and pepper to taste.

Ladle into warmed soup bowls. Heat the remaining olive oil in a small frying pan/skillet, add the sliced garlic and sauté carefully until just golden. Stir in the rosemary and dried chilli/hot pepper flakes. Dip the base of the frying pan/skillet in cold water to stop the garlic cooking. Spoon the garlic and oil over the soup, sprinkle with parsley and serve immediately.

Spinach broth with egg and cheese

Minestra di spinaci, uova e parmigiano

A typical way to thicken and enrich a broth in many parts of Italy is to add beaten eggs. This is one of the best I have tasted because of the freshness of the greens. Although most of us are limited to spinach, there are many more varieties of greens (ortaggi) in Italian markets and greengrocers – beet tops, for example, or even courgette/zucchini leaves and tendrils. Just outside Modena, this soup was rustled up in minutes for me, as I had arrived too late for anything else. Served with a basket of crusty bread and some homemade salami afterwards, it was just perfect.

700 g/1 lb. 9 oz. fresh spinach
60 g/4 tablespoons unsalted butter
4 very fresh eggs
5 tablespoons freshly grated Parmesan
¼ teaspoon freshly grated nutmeg
about 1.75 litres/7 cups good quality
    chicken stock
sea salt and freshly ground black pepper

Serves 6

Remove all the stalks from the spinach, then wash the leaves thoroughly – do not shake them dry. Cook the leaves in a large saucepan with the water still clinging. When the leaves have wilted, drain well, then chop finely.

Heat the butter in a medium saucepan, then add the spinach, tossing well to coat with the butter. Remove from the heat and let cool for 5 minutes.

Put the eggs, Parmesan, nutmeg, salt and pepper in a bowl and beat well. Mix into the chopped spinach.

Put the stock in a separate larger saucepan and bring almost to the boil. When almost boiling, whisk in the spinach and egg mixture as quickly as you can to avoid curdling. Reheat gently without boiling for a couple of minutes, ladle into warmed soup bowls and serve immediately.

Picking wild mushrooms is a late-summer-to-autumn/fall passion for all Italians, and for me in my native Scotland, with the porcino ('little pig' or Boletus edulis) being the most prized. In the Chianti hills or in Umbria, you can drive up winding country roads and see cars tucked into the bushes along the way, but you hardly ever see a person as everyone is deep in the undergrowth searching for mushrooms! Wild mushrooms have a strong, earthy, almost meaty taste and are piled high on a display table in a trattoria I love near Civitella in Tuscany. The combination of creamy chickpeas and earthy mushrooms is unusual and absolutely captivating – very 'Umbro-Toscano'.

Cream of chickpea soup with wild mushrooms

Crema di ceci ai porcini

25 g/1 oz. dried porcini mushrooms

60 g/4 tablespoons butter

50 g/2 oz. dry-cure smoked bacon cubes (*cubetti di pancetta*)

150 g/6 oz. fresh wild mushrooms

2 shallots, finely chopped

2 garlic cloves, coarsely chopped

freshly squeezed juice of 1 lemon

400-g/14-oz. can chickpeas, drained and rinsed

1.5 litres/6 cups good quality chicken or vegetable stock

150 ml/⅔ cup double/heavy cream

3 tablespoons chopped fresh flat-leaf parsley

sea salt and freshly ground black pepper

Serves 6

Put the dried porcini mushrooms in warm water and leave for 20 minutes, until softened.

Put the butter in a large saucepan, melt gently, then add the pancetta and sauté slowly until golden.

Put both the fresh and soaked dried mushrooms, shallots and garlic in a food processor and chop finely, using the pulse button. Add the mushroom mixture to the pancetta and cook, stirring over medium/high heat, for about 15 minutes, until all the juices have evaporated and the mixture becomes a thick paste. Stir in the lemon juice and chickpeas. Whisk in the stock and bring to the boil. Cover and simmer for about 25 minutes.

Transfer the soup, in batches if necessary, to a blender or food processor and blend until smooth. Return the soup to the rinsed-out pan and stir in the cream. Add salt and pepper to taste, then stir in the parsley (reserving a little to garnish) and reheat without boiling, or the soup may curdle. Ladle into warmed soup bowls, sprinkle with the reserved parsley and serve immediately.

Venetian fresh pea and rice soup with mint

Risi e bisi con la menta

This is a lovely soup to serve in the summer when fresh peas and mint are plentiful. Vialone nano is the favourite risotto rice in the Veneto region. It is a semi-fino round grain rice, best for soups and risotto, but arborio (a superfino used mainly for risotto) will do very nicely. This dish has very ancient roots, and was flavoured with fennel seeds at one time. Parsley is the usual addition now, but I prefer mint in the summer.

1.25 litres/5 cups chicken, good quality beef or vegetable stock

2 tablespoons olive oil

60 g/4 tablespoons butter

50 g/2 oz. dry-cure smoked bacon cubes (*cubetti di pancetta*)

1 large spring onion/scallion, finely chopped

200 g/1 cup Italian risotto rice

1 kg/2 lbs. fresh peas in the pod, shelled, or 400 g/2 cups frozen petit pois

3 tablespoons chopped fresh mint

freshly grated Parmesan, to serve

sea salt and freshly ground black pepper

Serves 4

Put the stock in a large saucepan and bring it slowly to the boil while you prepare the sautéed sauce (*soffrito*).

Heat the olive oil and half of the butter in a large saucepan and, when melted, add the pancetta and spring onion/scallion. Cook for about 5 minutes, until softened but not browned.

Add the rice, stir for a few minutes just to toast it, then add the hot stock. Simmer for 10 minutes, stirring from time to time. Add the peas, cook for another 5–7 minutes, then stir in the remaining butter and the mint. The rice grains should not be too mushy, and the soup should be thick, but not stodgy. Add salt and pepper to taste, ladle into warmed soup bowls and serve immediately with Parmesan for sprinkling.

Italy produces wonderful, comforting soups and this one from Campania combines two of the great stand-bys – beans and pasta. This is real trattoria stuff, and brings a smile of nostalgia to the face of any homesick Italian. I think it's because they remember nonna's version more than one from a trattoria!

Pasta and bean soup — Pasta e fagioli

185 g/1 generous cup dried cannellini or haricot beans

a pinch of bicarbonate of soda/baking soda

4 tablespoons olive oil, plus extra to serve

2 garlic cloves, crushed

1.75 litres/7 cups good quality chicken stock or water

100 g/1 cup short pasta shapes, such as *maccheroni* or *tubetti*

4 tomatoes, skinned, deseeded and coarsely chopped

4 tablespoons chopped fresh flat-leaf parsley

sea salt and freshly ground black pepper

Serves 6

Put the beans in a bowl, cover with cold water, add the bicarbonate of soda/baking soda and leave to soak overnight.

The next day, drain the beans and put them in a large saucepan. Add the olive oil, garlic and stock or water. Bring to the boil, reduce the heat and simmer, part-covered with a lid, for 1–2 hours, until the beans are tender.

Working in batches if necessary, blend the beans with the cooking liquid using a blender or food processor. Return the bean purée to the rinsed-out pan, adding extra water or stock as necessary.

Add the pasta and simmer gently for 15 minutes, until tender. (Add a little extra water or stock if the soup is too thick.) Stir in the tomatoes and parsley and season well with salt and pepper. Ladle into warmed soup bowls, drizzle some olive oil over the top and serve immediately.

Pasta, gnocchi and polenta

Fresh egg pasta Pasta all'uovo

Nothing beats homemade pasta. The texture is silky and the cooked dough itself very light. These quantities are only guidelines – depending on humidity and type of flour used, you may have to add more or less flour. I like to use a mixture of 50% Italian '00' flour and 50% Farina di Semola (pale yellow, finely ground, hard durum wheat flour). This mixture of flours gives the dough a firmer texture. You may also use strong white bread flour. The dough must not be too soft – it should require some serious effort when kneading! However, too much extra flour will make the pasta too tough to handle and when cooked, taste floury. Make a large batch and once cut and shaped you can freeze what you do not use. I prefer to make the dough by hand – if you use a food processor you can end up with a gloopy mess or little dry bullets.

200 g/1½ cups plain/all-purpose
  white flour (or use Italian '00'
  flour, see recipe intro)

2 medium eggs

a pinch of sea salt

1 tablespoon olive oil

a pasta machine (optional)

*Serves 2–4, depending
on size of portion*

TO MAKE THE PASTA THE TRADITIONAL WAY, sift the flour onto a clean work surface and make a well in the centre with your fist. Break the eggs into the well and add a pinch of salt and the oil. Gradually mix the eggs into the flour with the fingers of one hand, and bring it together into a firm dough. If the dough looks too dry, add a few drops of water, if too wet add more flour. Knead the pasta until smooth, lightly massage it with a hint of olive oil, pop into a polythene food bag and allow to rest for at least 30 minutes before rolling out. The pasta will be much more elastic after resting. Roll out by hand with a wooden rolling pin or use a pasta machine.

USING A PASTA MACHINE

Feed the rested dough 4–5 times through the widest setting of a pasta machine, folding in three each time, and feeding the open ends through the rollers to push out any air. This will finish the kneading process and make the pasta silky smooth.

Next, pass the pasta through the machine, starting at the widest setting first, then reducing the settings, one by one, until reaching the required thickness. The pasta sheet will become very long – so if you are having trouble, cut in it two and feed each half separately.

Generally the second from last setting is best for tagliatelle, the finest being for ravioli or pasta that is to be filled – but this depends on your machine.

Once the required thickness is reached, hang the pasta over a broom handle or the back of a chair to dry a little – this will make cutting it easier in humid weather, as it will not be so sticky. Alternatively, dust with a little flour and lay out flat on clean kitchen towels.

Tagliatelle: Roll the pasta dough out thinly on a lightly floured surface or roll out using a pasta machine. Roll or fold one end loosely towards the centre of the sheet, then do the same with the other so that they almost meet in the middle. Lift one folded side on top of the other – do not press down on the fold. Working quickly and deftly with one motion, cut into thin slices with a sharp knife, down the length of the folded pasta. Immediately unravel the slices to reveal the pasta ribbons – you can do this by inserting the back of a large knife and shaking them loose. Hang to dry a little before cooking or dust well with semolina flour and arrange in loose 'nests' on a basket or a tray lined with a clean kitchen towel.

Pappardelle: Roll out the pasta dough thinly on a lightly floured surface or roll out using a pasta machine. Using a fluted pastry wheel, cut into wide ribbons. Hang up to dry a little before cooking.

Tortellini: Roll out the pasta dough thinly on a lightly floured surface or roll out using a pasta machine. Using a round cookie cutter, stamp out rounds of pasta. Pipe or spoon your chosen filling into the middle of each round. Brush the edges with beaten egg and carefully fold the round, excluding all air. Bend the two corners round to form a crescent shape. Press to seal. Repeat with the remaining dough. Leave to dry on a floured kitchen towel for 30 minutes before cooking.

Ravioli: Cut the dough in half and wrap one half in clingfilm/plastic wrap. Roll out the pasta thinly on a lightly floured surface or roll out using a pasta machine. Cover with a kitchen towel and repeat with the remaining dough. Spoon small mounds of filling in even rows, spacing them at 4-cm/1 1/2 inch intervals across one piece of the dough. Using a pastry brush, brush the spaces of dough between the mounds with beaten egg. Using a rolling pin, lift the remaining sheet of pasta over the mounds. Press down firmly between the pockets of filling, pushing out any trapped air. Cut into squares with a serrated ravioli cutter or sharp knife. Transfer to a floured kitchen towel to rest for about 1 hour before cooking.

Macaroni: In Italy macaroni is the generic term for any hollow pasta shape. This simple-to-make version is called 'garganelle'. Roll the pasta out thinly to a rectangle on a lightly floured surface or roll out using a pasta machine. Cut squares from the pasta sheets and wrap around a pencil or chopstick on the diagonal to form tubes. Slip off and allow to dry slightly on a floured kitchen cloth before cooking.

Flavoured pastas

Follow the basic Fresh Egg Pasta recipe (see left) with the following additions:

Spinach Cook 150 g/5 oz. of frozen leaf spinach and squeeze out all the moisture. Blend with 1 medium egg until very smooth and season with salt and pepper.

Tomato Add 2 tablespoons tomato purée/paste or sun-dried tomato paste to the well in the flour. Use 1 large egg instead of 2 medium ones.

Beetroot/beet Add 2 tablespoons grated cooked beetroot/beet to the well in the flour. Use 1 large egg instead of 2 medium ones.

Saffron pasta Soak a sachet/package of powdered saffron in 2 tablespoons hot water for 15 minutes. Use 1 large egg instead of 2 medium ones and whisk in the saffron water.

Herb Add 3 tablespoons finely chopped fresh green herbs to the well in the flour.

Black squid ink Add 1 sachet of squid ink to the eggs before adding to the flour.

pasta, gnocchi and polenta **43**

I have eaten many variations of this dish in Sicily. It is very rich, but this is balanced by grated ricotta salata – ewe's milk ricotta cheese, salted and aged. It is very dry and concentrated, but sharp and salty. The nearest thing I can find to it outside the area is aged pecorino or even Greek feta cheese. Although a very ancient dish, it has been named 'alla Norma' by the people of Catania in homage to the composer Vincenzo Bellini, after one of his operas.

Spaghetti with aubergine and tomato sauce

Pasta alla norma

3 aubergines/eggplants (round violet ones if available)

500 g/1 lb. very ripe red tomatoes (add 2 tablespoons tomato purée/paste if not red enough)

3 tablespoons olive oil

3 garlic cloves, chopped

350 g/12 oz. spaghetti or spaghettini

3 tablespoons chopped fresh basil

3–4 tablespoons freshly grated *ricotta salata*, aged pecorino or Parmesan, plus extra to serve

vegetable oil, for sautéing

sea salt and freshly ground black pepper

Serves 4

Cut the aubergines/eggplants into small cubes and put in a colander. Sprinkle with salt and put the colander on a plate. Set aside to drain for 30 minutes.

Dip the tomatoes in boiling water for 10 seconds, then drop into cold water. Slip off the skins, cut in half, squeeze out and discard the seeds and chop the flesh coarsely. Heat the olive oil in a frying pan/skillet, add the garlic and cook for about 2–3 minutes until just golden, then add the tomatoes. Cook for 15 minutes more, until the tomatoes start to disintegrate.

Bring a large saucepan of lightly salted water to the boil, add the spaghetti and cook according to the packet instructions. Meanwhile, rinse the aubergines/eggplants, drain and pat dry with paper towels.

Heat 3 cm/1¼ inches vegetable oil in a frying pan/skillet, add the cubes of aubergine/eggplant and shallow fry until deep golden brown. Remove and drain on paper towels. Stir into the tomato sauce.

Drain the spaghetti, reserving 2 tablespoons of the cooking water in the pan and returning the pasta to the hot pan. Stir in the sauce, basil and grated cheese and serve immediately with more cheese on the side.

Long pasta is the choice for seafood dishes around coastal Italy – specifically spaghetti and spaghettini in the south. This is a simple dish made with local ingredients – nothing sophisticated, but so good. When buying mussels, make sure that when you tap each one sharply against the work surface it closes – if not, it is dead and should be thrown away. It's a good idea to soak the mussels in cold water overnight to purify them before cleaning them. This dish is equally good made with small clams.

Spaghetti with mussels, tomatoes and parsley

Spaghetti con le cozze

1 kg/2 lbs. live mussels or
    small clams

4 tablespoons olive oil

300 ml/scant 1¼ cups dry
    white wine

500 g/1 lb. spaghetti or spaghettini

2 garlic cloves, crushed

400-g/14-oz. can chopped
    tomatoes

2 tablespoons chopped fresh
    flat-leaf parsley

sea salt and freshly ground
    black pepper

Serves 4

Put the mussels in a bowl of cold water and rinse several times to remove any grit or sand. Pull off the beards and scrub well, discarding any that are not firmly closed. Drain.

Heat the oil and wine in a large saucepan and add the mussels. Stir over high heat until the mussels open. Remove and discard any that don't open.

Lift out the cooked mussels with a slotted spoon and put them in a bowl. Reserve the liquid. Cook the spaghetti in plenty of unsalted boiling water according to the packet instructions.

Meanwhile, add the garlic to the mussel cooking liquid in the pan and boil fast to concentrate the flavour. Stir in the tomatoes, return to the boil and boil fast for a further 3–4 minutes, until reduced. Stir in the mussels and half the parsley and heat through. Taste and season well with salt and pepper.

Drain the spaghetti, reserving 2 tablespoons of the cooking water in the pan. Return the pasta to the hot pan and stir in the sauce. Sprinkle with the remaining parsley and serve immediately.

Little alpine caps
Cappelletti degli alpini

I was so intrigued when I saw this on the menu of a family-run trattoria specializing in all sorts of game and mushroom dishes, in the mountains around Aosta, that I had to have them. A dish of perfectly formed, spinach pasta 'William Tell' hats appeared on my plate. They were filled with herb-scented capriolo (roebuck), and were dressed simply with olive oil. They were divine, and this is my re-creation using the more accessible cooked beef and pork.

1 quantity Fresh Egg Pasta, Spinach Pasta variation (see pages 42–43)

Filling
115 g/4 oz. cooked roast beef, coarsely chopped

150 g/6 oz. cooked roast pork, coarsely chopped

3 tablespoons freshly grated Parmesan

1 tablespoon chopped fresh thyme

2 juniper berries, crushed

freshly grated nutmeg

2 tablespoons fresh breadcrumbs

1 large egg

sea salt and freshly ground black pepper

To serve
400 ml/1¾ cups hot beef broth

extra virgin olive oil

freshly grated Parmesan

a pasta machine (optional)

Serves 4

To make the filling, put the beef and pork in a food processor with the Parmesan, thyme, juniper, nutmeg, breadcrumbs, egg, salt and pepper and pulse until finely chopped. Cover and set aside while you roll out the pasta.

Cut the rested pasta dough in half and roll each into a thin sheet. If you are using a pasta machine, roll to the second last setting. Cut the rolled-out pasta into at least twenty 10-cm/4-inch squares and dust with a little flour.

Take 1 square and cover the rest with clingfilm/plastic wrap. Put a small teaspoon of filling in the middle of the square. Dampen the edges with a wet pastry brush and fold a corner over the filling to meet the opposite corner to form a triangle. Press the edges together to seal, excluding any air. With the long edge towards you, bring the 2 points at either end of the edge together and overlap very slightly. Press together to seal. That's basically the shape – you can turn up a brim if you like. Set each one on a lightly floured kitchen towel. Repeat with the remaining filling and pasta.

Bring a large saucepan of lightly salted water to the boil. Add the pasta and cook for 3 minutes until puffy. Drain well, then carefully arrange in 4 warmed pasta plates, pour over the hot broth and serve with a drizzle of olive oil and Parmesan for sprinkling.

Ravioli pillows with potato and mozzarella

Guanciali di patate e mozzarella

It's surprising how popular potato-filled pasta is – I had never imagined it until a friend took me to a little restaurant where her mother did the cooking. This is the ultimate comfort food, with a hidden cube of melting mozzarella flowing out of the middle. You could add all sorts of things to the potatoes – such as chopped capers or olives – but I prefer it as it is. If the herb sauce doesn't appeal, serve the ravioli in meat or chicken broth, or with a thin meat sauce, such as the ragù on page 53.

2 quantities Fresh Egg Pasta
(see page 42)

Potato filling

500 g/1 lb. potatoes, unpeeled

50 g/3 tablespoons butter, cubed

50 g/½ cup freshly grated Parmesan, plus extra to serve

¼ teaspoon freshly grated nutmeg

1 egg, plus 1 egg yolk, beaten

2 tablespoons chopped fresh flat-leaf parsley

200 g/7 oz. fresh mozzarella, cut into 1.25 cm/¾ inch cubes (to give about 20)

sea salt and freshly ground black pepper

Herb sauce

115 g/1 stick unsalted butter

4 tablespoons mixed chopped fresh rosemary, thyme and parsley

sea salt and freshly ground black pepper

a piping bag fitted with a 1-cm/½-inch plain nozzle

a pasta machine (optional)

a serrated ravioli or pastry cutter (optional)

Serves 4

To make the filling, put the whole potatoes in a large saucepan of cold water and bring to the boil. Simmer for about 30 minutes, until they are completely tender when pierced to the centre with a skewer. Drain, then holding them in a clean kitchen towel, peel off the skin. Press through a potato ricer or sieve/strainer.

Mix the potatoes in a bowl with the butter, grated Parmesan and nutmeg. Beat in the eggs and parsley and season with salt and pepper. Fill the piping bag with the mixture.

Cut the rested pasta dough into 4 and roll each into a thin sheet. If you are using a pasta machine, roll to the second last setting. Put a piece of pasta on a lightly floured work surface, keeping the other pieces covered with clingfilm/plastic wrap. Pipe small lengths of potato about 4 cm/1½ inch long in even rows spacing them at 4-cm/1¾-inch intervals across one piece of the dough. Press a cube of mozzarella in the middle of each strip of potato. Using a pastry brush, brush water along the spaces between the mounds of filling, being careful not to wet the work surface or the dough might stick. Using a rolling pin, lift a second sheet of pasta over the dough covered with filling. Press down firmly between the mounds of filling, pushing out any trapped air. Cut into pillow-shaped rectangles with the ravioli cutter or a sharp knife. Transfer to a lightly floured kitchen towel. Repeat with the remaining filling, mozzarella and pasta.

To make the sauce, melt the butter in a saucepan with the herbs and season well with salt and pepper. Bring a large saucepan of lightly salted water to the boil. Add the ravioli and cook for 3 minutes until puffy. Drain well and toss with the herb sauce. Serve immediately with freshly grated Parmesan.

Oven-baked lasagne lasagne al forno

The classic version of this dish is pasta layered with meat sauce (ragù) and creamy bechamel sauce (salsa besciamella). It is very easy to assemble and you can make the meat sauce the day before, and the béchamel sauce on the day. If you use fresh pasta, it doesn't need precooking, and is layered up as it is. Just make sure the ragù is quite liquid as this will be absorbed into the pasta as it cooks.

about 12 sheets of dried lasagne or made from Fresh Egg Pasta, Spinach Pasta variation (see pages 42–43) rolled out to the second last setting on the pasta machine

about 50 g/½ cup freshly grated Parmesan

Ragù

75 g/3 oz. dry-cure smoked bacon, such as pancetta, in a piece

100 g/4 oz. chicken livers (optional)

50 g/4 tablespoons butter

1 onion, finely chopped

1 carrot, chopped

1 celery stalk/rib, finely chopped

250 g/9 oz. minced/ground beef (as lean as possible)

2 tablespoons tomato purée/paste

100 ml/⅓ cup dry white wine

200 ml/¾ cup good quality beef stock or water

freshly grated nutmeg

sea salt and freshly ground black pepper

Béchamel sauce

150 g/1¼ sticks unsalted butter

110 g/1 cup plain/all-purpose white flour

about 1 litre/4 cups milk

sea salt

a deep, rectangular baking dish, about 25 x 20 cm/10 x 8 inches, well buttered

Serves 4—6

To make the ragù, cut the pancetta into small cubes. Trim the chicken livers (if using), removing any fat or gristle. Cut off any discoloured bits, which will be bitter if left on. Coarsely chop the livers.

Melt the butter in a saucepan, add the pancetta and cook for 2–3 minutes until browning. Add the onion, carrot and celery and brown these too. Stir in the minced/ground beef and brown until just changing colour, but not hardening – break it up with a wooden spoon. Stir in the chicken livers and cook for 2–3 minutes. Add the tomato purée/paste, mix well and pour in the wine and stock. Season well with nutmeg, salt and pepper. Bring to the boil, cover and simmer very gently for as long as you can – 2 hours if possible.

To make the béchamel sauce, melt the butter in a large saucepan. When foaming, add the flour and cook over gentle heat for about 5 minutes without letting it brown. Have a balloon whisk ready. Slide off the heat and add all the milk at once, whisking very well. When all the flour and butter have been amalgamated and there are no lumps, return to the heat and slowly bring to the boil, whisking all the time. When it comes to the boil, add salt, simmer gently for 2–3 minutes, then use immediately.

If making in advance, cover the surface directly with clingfilm/plastic wrap to prevent a skin forming, then let cool. When reheating, remove the clingfilm/plastic wrap and reheat very gently, stirring every now and then until liquid. Don't worry too much about lumps – they will disappear when the whole dish cooks. If you like a thinner sauce, just add extra milk after it has boiled and thickened.

When ready to assemble, cook the sheets of dried lasagne in plenty of boiling water in batches according to the packet instructions. Lift out with a slotted spoon and drain on a clean kitchen towel. Fresh pasta will not need cooking. Spoon one-third of the meat sauce into the prepared baking dish. Cover with 4 sheets of lasagne and spread with one-third of the béchamel. Repeat twice more, finishing with a layer of béchamel covering the whole top. Sprinkle with Parmesan. Bake in a preheated oven at 180°C (350°F) Gas 4 for about 45 minutes, until brown and bubbling. Let stand for 10 minutes to settle and firm up before serving.

VARIATIONS: You could vary the recipe by using grated mozzarella instead of the béchamel, or by mixing ricotta, spinach, chopped sun-dried tomatoes, Parmesan and herbs together instead of the meat sauce. Traditional ragù contains chicken livers to add richness, but you can leave them out and replace with an additional quantity of minced/ground beef or pork, if preferred.

Gnocchi with rocket pesto

Gnocchi di patate con pesto di rucola e noci

Classic gnocchi originate in northern Italy, where they are a staple food. They are served just with melted butter and Parmesan or a tomato sauce, but they are delicious with pesto made from peppery rocket/arugula and walnuts. They must be made with a good floury potato to give them lightness: they should be puffy pillows of potato. It takes a little practice to make gnocchi really light, as overworking makes them tough.

1 kg/2 lbs. floury potatoes, unpeeled

1 teaspoon sea salt

50 g/4 tablespoons butter, melted

1 small egg, beaten

225–275 g/1½–1¼ cups plain/all-purpose white flour

Parmesan shavings, to serve

Rocket pesto

100 g/4 oz. rocket/arugula leaves

2–3 garlic cloves

finely grated zest of 1 lemon

50 g/½ cup shelled walnuts

200 ml/¾ cup extra virgin olive oil, plus extra to cover

50 g/½ cup finely grated Parmesan

sea salt and freshly ground black pepper

Serves 4

To make the gnocchi, cook the unpeeled potatoes in boiling water for 20–30 minutes until very tender; drain well.

Meanwhile, to make the pesto, put the rocket/arugula, garlic, lemon zest, walnuts, olive oil, Parmesan, salt and pepper in a food processor and blend until it is the texture you want. Scrape out into a jar, level the surface and pour in enough olive oil to cover.

Halve the potatoes and press through a potato ricer, or peel and press through a sieve/strainer into a bowl. While they are still warm, add the 1 teaspoon salt, the butter, beaten egg and half the flour. Mix lightly, then transfer to a floured board. Gradually knead in enough of the remaining flour to yield a smooth, soft, slightly sticky dough. Roll the dough into thick sausages, 2.5 cm/1 inch in diameter. Cut into 2-cm/¾-inch pieces and shape into corks or pull each one down over the back of a fork to produce the traditional ridged outside and the concave inside. Put them on a lightly floured kitchen towel.

Bring a large saucepan of salted water to the boil. Cook the gnocchi in batches. Drop them into the boiling water and cook for 2–3 minutes or until they float to the surface. Remove with a slotted spoon immediately they rise and keep hot while you cook the remainder. Toss with the pesto and serve immediately, topped with Parmesan shavings.

NOTE The pesto can be stored in a jar, covered with a layer of oil and in the refrigerator for up to 2 weeks.

Soft and golden, these gnocchi are a staple in the Lazio area around Rome. I have added herbs and mustard to the basic mix and like to serve them with roasted rabbit or lamb. They are most often are served with a tomato sauce and are a great favourite with children. Did you know that semolina is hard wheat (durum), ground slightly coarser than flour? It is not a special grain on its own.

Roman gnocchi with herbs and semolina

Gnocchi alla romana con le erbe

1 litre/4 cups milk

250 g/1⅔ cups semolina

175 g/1¾ cups freshly grated
   Parmesan

115 g/1 stick butter

2 egg yolks

1 tablespoon Dijon mustard

2 tablespoons chopped fresh sage

3 tablespoons chopped fresh
   flat-leaf parsley

sea salt and freshly ground
   black pepper

*a baking sheet lined with
   clingfilm/plastic wrap*

a 5-cm/2-inch cookie cutter

*a rectangular, baking dish,
   25 x 20 cm/10 x 8 inches,
   well buttered*

Pour the milk into a saucepan and whisk in the semolina. Bring slowly to the boil, stirring all the time until it really thickens – about 10 minutes (it should be quite thick, like choux pastry dough). Beat in half the Parmesan, half the butter, the egg yolks, mustard, sage and parsley. Add salt and pepper to taste.

Spread the mixture onto the prepared baking sheet to a depth of about 1 cm/½ inch. Set aside for about 2 hours, until cool and set.

Preheat the oven to 200°C (400°F) Gas 6. Stamp out shapes from the cooled gnocchi with the cookie cutter. Spread the chopped trimmings in the bottom of the prepared baking dish. Dot with some of the remaining butter and sprinkle with a little grated Parmesan. Arrange the gnocchi shapes in a single layer over the trimmings. Dot with the remaining butter and Parmesan. Bake in the preheated oven for 20–25 minutes, until golden and crusty. Let stand for 5 minutes before serving.

Serves 4—6

Soft polenta with sausage ragù

Polenta con ragù di salsiccia

This is a real winter-warmer from the north of Italy, where polenta is the staple carbohydrate. I have been to a polenta night where the steaming soft cereal was poured straight onto a huge wooden board set in the middle of the table. The sauce was poured into a large hollow in the centre of the polenta and everyone gathered round to help themselves directly from the pile – no plates necessary. This is still done in some mountain trattorie.

2 teaspoons sea salt

300 g/2 cups instant polenta

freshly grated Parmesan, to serve

Sausage ragù

500 g/1lb. fresh Italian pork sausages or good all-meat pork sausages

2 tablespoons olive oil

1 onion, finely chopped

500 ml/2 cups passata (Italian strained tomatoes)

150 ml/⅔ cup dry red wine

6 sun-dried tomatoes in oil, drained and sliced

sea salt and freshly ground black pepper

Serves 4

To make the ragù, squeeze the sausage meat out of the skins into a bowl and break up the meat.

Heat the oil in a medium saucepan and add the onion. Cook for 5 minutes until soft and golden. Stir in the sausage meat, browning it all over and breaking up the lumps with a wooden spoon. Pour in the passata and the wine. Bring to the boil. Add the sun-dried tomatoes and simmer for about 30 minutes, until well reduced, stirring occasionally. Add salt and pepper to taste.

Meanwhile, bring 1.4 litres/5½ cups water to the boil with 2 teaspoons salt. Sprinkle in the polenta, stirring or whisking to prevent lumps forming.

Simmer for 5–10 minutes, stirring constantly, until thickened like soft mashed potato. Quickly spoon the polenta into 4 large, warmed soup plates and make a hollow in the centre of each. Top with the sausage ragù and serve with grated Parmesan.

Baked polenta with fontina and pancetta

Polenta pasticciata alla valdostana

Say 'alla Valdostana', and every Italian will know that there's Fontina cheese in the dish. This is one of the oldest cheeses made in the Valle d'Aosta – it is rich and nutty and melts very easily. It is also the basis of a type of fondue called fonduta. This polenta dish is typical fare in some of the little family restaurants you come across off-piste when skiing in the mountains. Sometimes it comes with a wild mushroom or venison sauce. Just the stuff to keep out the cold and set you on your way.

300 g/2 cups instant polenta (or real polenta/cornmeal flour)

350 g/12 oz. Fontina, raclette, or a mixture of grated mozzarella and Cheddar

100 g/1 cup freshly grated Parmesan

175 g/6 oz. thinly sliced pancetta or other dry-cure smoked bacon

sea salt and freshly ground black pepper

a shallow baking dish, 25 x 20 cm/ 10 x 8 inches, buttered

Serves 6

If using instant polenta, cook according to the packet instructions, then turn out into a mound on a wooden board and let cool and set.

To make real polenta, bring 1 litre/4 cups salted water to the boil, then slowly sprinkle in the polenta flour through your fingers, whisking all the time to stop lumps. Cook, stirring with a wooden spoon, for 45 minutes on low heat and then turn out into a mound on a wooden board and let cool and set.

Preheat the oven to 180°C (350°F) Gas 4. Slice the Fontina thinly or grate it. Cut the polenta into slices about 1 cm/½ inch thick. Arrange a layer of polenta in the prepared baking dish. Top with half the Fontina and half the Parmesan. Add another layer of polenta, then cover with the remaining Fontina and the remaining Parmesan. Finally, add a layer of pancetta.

Bake in the preheated oven for about 40 minutes, until brown and bubbling and the pancetta is crisp on top. Let stand for 5 minutes before serving.

Risotto

Parmesan and butter risotto Risotto alla parmigiana

When you have nothing except risotto rice in the cupboard, and a chunk of Parmesan and some butter in the refrigerator, yet feel the need for comfort and luxury, this is the risotto for you. It is pale, golden, smooth and creamy and relies totally on the quality of the rice, butter and cheese. I would use real Parmigiano Reggiano, with its sweet, nutty flavour, and nothing else.

about 1.5 litres/6 cups hot, good
  quality chicken or vegetable
  stock
150 g/1¼ sticks unsalted butter
1 onion, finely chopped
500 g/2½ cups Italian risotto rice
150 ml/⅔ cup dry white wine
100 g/1 cup freshly grated
  Parmesan
sea salt and freshly ground
  black pepper

Serves 4—6

Put the stock in a saucepan and keep at a gentle simmer. Melt about half the butter in a large, heavy saucepan and add the onion. Cook gently for about 10 minutes until soft, golden and translucent but not browned. Add the rice and stir until well coated with the butter and heated through. Pour in the wine and boil hard until it has reduced and almost disappeared.

Begin adding the stock, a large ladleful at a time, stirring gently until each one has almost been absorbed by the rice. The risotto should be kept at a bare simmer throughout cooking, so don't let the rice dry out – add more stock as necessary. Continue for about 15–20 minutes, until the rice is tender and creamy, but the grains still firm.

Taste and season well with salt and pepper, then stir in the remaining butter and all the Parmesan. Cover and let rest for a couple of minutes so the risotto can relax and the cheese melt, then spoon into warmed serving bowls and serve immediately.

I live in Scotland and was tempted to make a traditional pumpkin risotto using what we call 'turnip' (swede) instead. I was impressed with the result. It was less sweet and cloying than it would be using pumpkin or squash, but had a very distinct flavour. I have served this on Burns' Night on 25th January with traditional Scottish haggis, and it is delicious – to my taste anyway – but stick to the traditional recipe and it will be just as good. This tastes wonderful on its own or served with barbecued lamb chops.

Butternut squash, sage and chilli risotto

Risotto alla zucca, salvia e peperoncino

about 1.5 litres/6 cups hot good quality chicken or vegetable stock

125 g/1 stick unsalted butter

1 large onion, finely chopped

1–2 fresh or dried red chillies/hot peppers, deseeded and finely chopped

500 g/1 lb. butternut squash or pumpkin (or swede/rutabaga), peeled and finely diced

500 g/2½ cups Italian risotto rice

3 tablespoons chopped fresh sage

75 g/¾ cup freshly grated Parmesan

sea salt and freshly ground black pepper

Serves 6

Put the stock in a saucepan and keep at a gentle simmer. Melt about half the butter in a large, heavy saucepan and add the onion. Cook gently for about 10 minutes until soft, golden and translucent but not browned. Stir in the chopped chillies/hot peppers and cook for 1 minute. Add the squash, and cook, stirring constantly over the heat for 5 minutes, until it begins to soften slightly. Stir in the rice and coat with the butter and vegetables. Cook for a few minutes to toast the grains.

Begin adding the stock, a large ladleful at a time, stirring gently until each one has almost been absorbed by the rice. The risotto should be kept at a bare simmer throughout cooking, so don't let the rice dry out – add more stock as necessary. Continue for about 15–20 minutes, until the rice is tender and creamy, but the grains still firm and the squash beginning to disintegrate.

Taste, season well with salt and pepper and stir in the sage, remaining butter and all the Parmesan. Cover, let rest for a couple of minutes, spoon into warmed serving bowls then serve immediately.

Mozzarella and sun-blushed tomato risotto with basil

Risotto con mozzarella e pomodori semi-secchi

When you dip your fork into this risotto, you will come across pockets of melting mozzarella. Mix in the tomato topping and you will make more strings. Try to use real mozzarella di bufala – it has a fresh, lactic bite, well suited to this recipe.

about 1.5 litres/6 cups
   hot good quality chicken
   or vegetable stock
125 g/1 stick unsalted butter
1 onion, finely chopped
400 g/2 cups Italian risotto rice
150 ml/⅔ cup dry white wine
250 g/9 oz. mozzarella, cut into
   1-cm/½-inch cubes
4 tablespoons chopped fresh basil
300 g/10 oz. sun-blushed tomatoes
sea salt and freshly ground
   black pepper

To serve

extra basil leaves
freshly grated Parmesan

Serves 4

Put the stock in a saucepan and keep at a gentle simmer. Melt about half the butter in a large, heavy saucepan and add the onion. Cook gently for about 10 minutes until soft, golden and translucent but not browned. Add the rice and stir until well coated with the butter and heated through. Pour in the wine and boil hard until it has reduced and almost disappeared.

Begin adding the stock, a large ladleful at a time, stirring gently until each one has almost been absorbed by the rice. The risotto should be kept at a bare simmer throughout cooking, so don't let the rice dry out – add more stock as necessary. Continue for about 15–20 minutes, until the rice is tender and creamy, but the grains still firm.

Taste and season well with salt and pepper and beat in the remaining butter. Fold in the cubed mozzarella and chopped basil.

Cover and let rest for a couple of minutes so the risotto can relax and the cheese melt. Spoon into warmed serving bowls and put a pile of tomatoes in the centre of each one. Top with basil leaves and serve immediately with grated Parmesan.

Artichoke and pecorino risotto

Risotto ai carciofi e pecorino

Smoky chargrilled artichokes are wonderful combined with nutty pecorino. Pecorino is made from ewe's milk (latte de pecora) and when aged can be grated like Parmesan. When young, it has a Cheddar-like texture and a rich, nutty flavour.

12 fresh artichokes or chargrilled deli artichokes

olive oil, for brushing

about 1.5 litres/6 cups hot good quality chicken or vegetable stock

125 g/1 stick unsalted butter

1 onion, finely chopped

500 g/2½ cups Italian risotto rice

150 ml/⅔ cup dry white wine

75 g/¾ cup freshly grated pecorino, plus extra to serve

sea salt and freshly ground black pepper

Serves 4

First prepare the fresh artichokes, if using (see below), then brush with olive oil and chargrill for 5 minutes on a stove-top grill pan/griddle, turning often. If using chargrilled ones from the deli, cut them in quarters and set aside.

Put the stock in a saucepan and keep at a gentle simmer. Melt about half of the butter in a large, heavy saucepan and add the onion. Cook gently for about 10 minutes until soft, golden and translucent but not browned. Add the rice and stir until well coated with the butter and heated through. Pour in the wine and boil hard until it has reduced and almost disappeared.

Begin adding the stock, a large ladleful at a time, stirring gently until each one has almost been absorbed by the rice. The risotto should be kept at a bare simmer throughout cooking, so don't let the rice dry out – add more stock as necessary. Continue for about 15–20 minutes, until the rice is tender and creamy, but the grains still firm.

Taste and season well with salt and pepper and beat in the remaining butter and all the pecorino. Fold in the artichokes. Cover and let rest for a couple of minutes so the risotto can relax. Spoon into warmed serving bowls then serve immediately with extra pecorino.

NOTE To prepare fresh artichokes, you will need 1 lemon, halved, and purple-green baby artichokes with stems and heads, about 10 cm/4 inches long. Fill a large bowl with water and squeeze in the juice of ½ lemon to acidulate it. Use the other lemon half to rub the cut portions of the artichoke as you work. Trim the artichokes by snapping off the dark outer leaves, starting at the base. Trim the stalk down to about 5 cm/2 inches. Trim away the green outer layer at the base and peel the fibrous outside of the stalk with a vegetable peeler. Cut about 1 cm/½ inch off the tip of each artichoke heart. Put each artichoke in the lemony water until needed – this will stop them discolouring. Drain and use as required.

Risotto with red wine, mushrooms and pancetta

Risotto al chianti, funghi e pancetta

Risotto made with red wine is a miracle of flavour combinations. The sweetness from the mushrooms and cheese and the smoky saltiness from the pancetta make this unforgettable. The important thing to remember here is to reduce the wine completely to boil off the alcohol and reduce the acidity. This is a risotto to make in the colder months, when you need big, comforting flavours.

65 ml/¼ cup olive oil or 75 g/
    5 tablespoons unsalted butter

75 g/3 oz. pancetta or other
    dry-cure smoked bacon,
    finely chopped

1 red onion, finely chopped

200 g/7 oz. cremini or porcini
    mushrooms, finely chopped

500 g/2½ cups Italian risotto rice

250 ml/1 cup good Chianti wine

about 1.5 litres/6 cups hot, good
    quality chicken or meat stock

100 g/1 cup freshly grated
    Parmesan

sea salt and freshly ground
    black pepper

To serve

1 large porcini mushroom, sliced
    and sautéed in olive oil until
    golden (optional)

2 tablespoons chopped fresh
    flat-leaf parsley

Serves 6

Heat half the oil or butter in a large saucepan and add the chopped pancetta, cook until the fat begins to run, then add the onion and mushrooms. Cook gently for 5 minutes, until softened and translucent.

Stir in the rice and cook for 1–2 minutes, until the rice smells toasty and looks opaque. Add the wine and boil hard until the liquid disappears.

Add a ladleful of hot stock and simmer, stirring until absorbed. Continue for about 15–20 minutes, adding the stock a ladleful at a time, until only 2 ladles of stock remain. The rice should be tender but still have some bite to it. As soon as the rice is tender, stir in the remaining olive oil or butter and all the Parmesan. Taste and season well with salt and pepper.

Finally, stir in the remaining stock and let stand with the lid on for 5 minutes. Spoon into warmed serving bowls, top with the sautéed porcini slices (if using), sprinkle with parsley and serve immediately.

Seafood and saffron risotto

Risotto ai frutti di mare

Central and northern Italy are the places to go for good risotto – I've never eaten a really good one in the south. Seafood risotto should be creamy and slightly soupy – what the Italians refer to as 'all'onda', meaning 'like a wave'. The best seafood risotti come from the Venice area, where seafood is abundant in the lagoons. Saffron gives a wonderful warm colour and musky flavour. Generally, you will never be offered Parmesan with a fish risotto – it is frowned upon, so don't ask!

1 teaspoon saffron threads

1.5 litres/6 cups good quality fish stock

300 ml/scant 1¼ cups dry white wine

350 g/12 oz. uncooked prawn/shrimp tails, unpeeled

6 baby squid, cleaned and cut into rings

6 fresh scallops, halved horizontally if large

500 g/1 lb. live mussels, cleaned (see Note on page 14)

250 g/9 oz. fresh baby/cherrystone clams (*vongole*), rinsed

3 tablespoons olive oil

1 onion, finely chopped

500 g/2½ cups Italian risotto rice

sea salt and freshly ground black pepper

3 tablespoons chopped fresh flat-leaf parsley, to serve

Serves 6

Put the saffron in a small bowl and cover with boiling water. Set aside to infuse while you cook the fish.

Pour the stock and wine into a large saucepan and heat to simmering point. Add the prawns/shrimp and cook for 2 minutes. Add the squid and scallops and cook for a further 2 minutes. Remove them with a slotted spoon and set aside.

Put the mussels and clams into the stock and bring to the boil. Cover and cook for 3–5 minutes, until all the shells have opened. Remove with a slotted spoon and set aside. Keep the stock hot.

Heat the oil in a separate large saucepan and add the onion. Sauté for 5 minutes, until softened and translucent. Stir in the rice and cook for 1–2 minutes, until the rice smells toasty and looks opaque. Add the saffron water and a ladleful of stock and simmer, stirring, until absorbed. Continue for about 18 minutes, adding the stock a ladleful at a time, until only 2 ladles of stock remain. The rice should be tender but still have some bite to it. Taste and season well with salt and pepper.

Finally, stir in the remaining stock and seafood and let stand with the lid on for 5 minutes. Spoon into warmed serving bowls, sprinkle with parsley and serve immediately.

Pizza and bread

The pizza maker's tomato sauce Salsa pizzaiola

Pizzaiola sauce is named after the traditional sauce that a pizza maker would put on the base of a pizza. To acquire its distinctive, concentrated, almost caramelized flavour, the tomatoes must cook at a very lively heat in a shallow pan.

8 tablespoons olive oil
2 garlic cloves, chopped
1 teaspoon dried oregano
800 g/1¾ lbs. fresh tomatoes, skinned and coarsely chopped or 2 x 400-g/14-oz cans chopped tomatoes
sea salt and freshly ground black pepper

Serves 4

Put the oil in a large shallow pan and heat almost to smoking point (a wok is good for this). Standing back (it will splutter if it's at the right temperature), add the garlic, oregano and tomatoes.

Cook over a fierce heat for 5–8 minutes or until the sauce is thick and glossy. Season with salt and pepper.

Pizza alla margherita

The recipe is for a Sicilian pizza dough and was given to me by a gravel-voiced pizzaiolo. He insists that using a touch of lemon juice in the dough (made with special finely ground semolina flour for making bread, pasta and pizzas) makes it light and crisp, and I have to agree. You can adapt this recipe to plain/all-purpose flour and it works very well, but the crust is not as golden. This is a very patriotic pizza topping – the three colours representing the Italian national flag.

1 quantity Pizza Maker's Tomato Sauce (see left)
250 g/9 oz. fresh mozzarella, thinly sliced
a large handful of fresh basil leaves
extra olive oil, for drizzling
sea salt and freshly ground black pepper

Sicilian pizza dough

250 g/1⅔ cups fine Italian semolina flour or durum wheat flour (see Note)
7 g/¼ oz compressed fresh yeast
1 tablespoon freshly squeezed lemon juice
1 tablespoon olive oil
a pinch of sea salt
about 300 ml/scant 1¼ cups warm water

a 'testo', terracotta bakestone or 2 large, heavy baking sheets
2 baking sheets lined with non-stick baking parchment
a baker's peel (optional)

Makes 2 thin-crust pizzas, each about 25 cm/10 inches diameter

Put the testo, bakestone or large, heavy baking sheets in the oven and preheat to 220°C (425°F) Gas 7.

To make the dough, put the semolina flour in a bowl, crumble the fresh yeast into the flour, add the lemon juice, olive oil and a generous pinch of salt, then add enough warm water to form a very soft dough. Transfer to a floured surface and knead for about 10 minutes, until smooth and elastic. Put the dough in a clean, oiled bowl (or an oiled polythene bag), cover and let rise for about 1 hour, until doubled in size.

Cut the dough in half and knead each half into a round. Pat or roll the rounds into 25-cm/10-inch circles, keeping the bases well floured. Transfer the pizzas onto the baking sheets lined with baking parchment. Spread each one lightly with the tomato sauce, cover with sliced mozzarella and season with salt and pepper. Let rise in a warm place for 10 minutes, then open the oven door, and slide both paper and pizza onto the hot testo, bakestone or baking sheets. If you are brave, try to shoot them into the oven so that they leave the paper behind – this takes practice! Alternatively, use a baker's peel, if you have one.

Bake for about 18–20 minutes, until the crust is golden and the cheese melted but still white. Remove from the oven, sprinkle with basil leaves and olive oil and serve immediately.

NOTE In Sicily, we make this with Italian *farina di semola*. It is very finely ground and needs no extra flour. You can grind ordinary semolina into fine flour by working it in a blender for about 2 minutes.

Potato pizza

Pizza con radicchio, patate e fontina

In general, Italians like to stick to the classics when it comes to pizza, but as you can see below, pizza toppings are limitless. I have taken inspiration from a dish I had in Verona, and applied it to a pizza – well, it's just bread and cheese after all, isn't it?

15 g/½ oz. compressed fresh yeast, 1 tablespoon active dried yeast or 7-g/¼-oz. sachet/package fast action dried yeast

a pinch of sugar

250 ml/1 cup warm water

350 g/2¼ cups plain/all-purpose white flour, plus extra for dusting

1 tablespoon olive oil

a pinch of sea salt

Potato topping

1 potato, peeled and sliced extremely thinly

150 g/6 oz. Fontina, Taleggio or mozzarella

1 large radicchio, cut into about 8 wedges, brushed with olive oil and grilled/broiled for 5 minutes

1 tablespoon chopped fresh thyme

sea salt and freshly ground black pepper

extra olive oil, for drizzling

a baking tin/pan, about 23 x 33 cm/9 x 13 inches

Serves 2—4

To make the dough, put the fresh yeast and sugar in a medium bowl and beat until creamy. Whisk in the warm water and leave for 10 minutes until frothy. For other yeasts, use according to the package instructions.

Sift the flour into a large bowl and make a well in the centre. Pour in the yeast mixture, olive oil and a good pinch of salt. Mix with a round-bladed knife, then your hands, until the dough comes together. Transfer to a floured surface, wash and dry your hands and knead for 10 minutes until smooth and elastic. The dough should be quite soft, but if too soft to handle, kneed in more flour, 1 tablespoon at a time. Put the dough in a clean, oiled bowl, cover with a damp kitchen towel or clingfilm/plastic wrap and let rise for about 1 hour, until doubled in size.

When risen, punch the dough down with your fists, then roll out or pat into a rectangle that will fit in the baking tin/pan, pushing it up the sides a little. Cover the top of the dough with a thin layer of sliced potato, then half the cheese, the wedges of radicchio, then the remaining cheese. Season with salt and pepper, and sprinkle with thyme. Drizzle oil over the top and let rise in a warm place for 10 minutes.

Meanwhile, preheat the oven to 220°C (425°F) Gas 7. Bake the pizza in the preheated oven for about 15–20 minutes, until golden and bubbling. Serve immediately.

Filled rustic pizzas

Pizza rustica

Italians are traditionally very thrifty, and a really good double-crust pizza can be put together with a carefully chosen mixture of leftovers. There must be cheese or béchamel sauce to keep it moist, but you can add anchovies, cooked meat sauce (ragù), capers or olives – whatever you like, as long as their flavours suit each other.

15 g/½ oz. compressed fresh yeast, 1 tablespoon active dried yeast or 7-g/¼-oz. sachet/package fast action dried yeast

a pinch of sugar

250 ml/1 cup warm water

350 g/2¼ cups plain/all-purpose white flour

1 tablespoon olive oil, plus extra for brushing

a pinch of sea salt

Filling

100 g/4 oz. mozzarella, cubed

100 g/4 oz. cubed salami or ham

50 g/2 oz. cooked chopped spinach

4 sun-dried tomatoes in oil, drained and chopped

3–4 tablespoons Pizza Maker's Tomato Sauce (see page 78) or any prepared tomato sauce

2–3 tablespoons chopped fresh green herbs (any mixture)

sea salt and freshly ground black pepper

a baking sheet, floured

Serves 2

To make the dough, put the fresh yeast and sugar in a medium bowl and beat until creamy. Whisk in the warm water and leave for 10 minutes until frothy. For other yeasts, use according to the package instructions.

Sift the flour into a large bowl and make a well in the centre. Pour in the yeast mixture, olive oil and a good pinch of salt. Mix with a round-bladed knife, then your hands, until the dough comes together. Transfer to a floured surface, wash and dry your hands and knead for 10 minutes until smooth and elastic. The dough should be quite soft, but if too soft to handle, knead in more flour, 1 tablespoon at a time. Put the dough in a clean, oiled bowl, cover with a damp kitchen towel or clingfilm/plastic wrap and let rise for about 1 hour, until doubled in size.

Preheat the oven to 220°C (425°F) Gas 7. To make the filling, put the mozzarella, salami, spinach, sun-dried tomatoes, tomato sauce and herbs in a bowl and season with salt and pepper.

Roll out the dough to a large circle, making sure it is well floured so it doesn't stick. Pile the filling onto one half of the dough, avoiding the edges. Flip over the other half to cover, press the edges together to seal, then twist and crimp. Slide onto the floured baking sheet and brush lightly with olive oil. Make a slash in the top or it could explode when cooking!

Bake in the preheated oven for about 25 minutes, until golden and firm. Remove from the oven, let sit for 5 minutes, then serve.

White pizza Pizza bianca

Neapolitans call pizza without tomatoes pizza bianca. All the flavour comes from the mozzarella, so this has to be the finest mozzarella di bufala. This recipe will make the typical Neapolitan pizza base – soft and chewy with a crisp crust.

100 g/4 oz. buffalo mozzarella (*mozzarella di bufala*)

a handful of small fresh sage leaves

sea salt and freshly ground black pepper

Neopolitan pizza dough

15 g/½ oz. compressed fresh yeast, 1 tablespoon active dried yeast or 7-g/¼-oz. sachet/package fast action dried yeast

½ teaspoon sugar

250 ml/1 cup hand-hot water

500 g/4 cups Italian '0' grade flour or unbleached plain/all-purpose flour, plus extra for dusting

1 teaspoon sea salt

1 tablespoon olive oil, plus extra for drizzling

a 'testo', terracotta bakestone or large, heavy baking sheet

a rimless baking sheet or baker's peel

non-stick baking parchment

Makes 1 medium-crust pizza, 25-cm / 10-inches diameter

To make the dough, put the fresh yeast and sugar in a medium bowl and beat until creamy. Whisk in the hand-hot water and leave for 10 minutes until frothy. For other yeasts, use according to the package instructions.

Sift the flour and salt into a large bowl and make a well in the centre. Pour in the yeast mixture, then the olive oil. Mix with a round-bladed knife, then use your hands until the dough comes together. Transfer to a lightly floured surface, then knead briskly for 5–10 minutes, until smooth, shiny and elastic. The dough should be quite soft – if you feel the dough is sticky, flour your hands, not the dough. Shape the dough into a neat ball. Put in an oiled bowl, cover with a damp kitchen towel and leave to rise in a warm draught-free place for about 1½ hours, until doubled in size. Uncover the dough, punch out the air, then tip out onto a lightly floured work surface. Shape into a smooth ball. Cover loosely with clingfilm/plastic wrap and leave to rise for another 1–1½ hours. Put the testo, bakestone or heavy baking sheet on the lower shelf of the oven. Preheat the oven to 220°C (425°F) Gas 7.

Lightly squeeze any excess moisture out of the mozzarella, then slice it and put it on paper towels for 5 minutes to absorb any remaining moisture.

Uncover the dough, punch out the air and roll or pull into a 25-cm/10-inch circle directly onto a sheet of baking parchment. Slide this onto the rimless baking sheet or baker's peel. Arrange the mozzarella evenly over the pizza base, leaving a 1-cm/½-inch rim around the edge. Scatter the sage over the cheese, then season and drizzle with olive oil. Working quickly, open the oven door and slide both paper and pizza onto the hot testo, bakestone or baking sheet. If you are brave, try to shoot the pizza into the oven so that it leaves the paper behind – this takes practice!

Bake for 5 minutes, then carefully slide out the paper. Bake the pizza for a further 15 minutes, until the crust is golden and the cheese melted and bubbling. Remove from the oven, sprinkle with cracked black pepper and serve immediately.

Calzone Calzone alla parmigiana

This is a good calzone to make for more than two people. The filling ingredients can be chopped as finely or roughly as you like, but the aubergine/eggplant must be cooked through before it goes into the dough.

1 quantity Neopolitan Pizza Dough (see page 84), up to the first rising

2 aubergines/eggplants, cubed

12 whole garlic cloves, peeled

4 tablespoons extra virgin olive oil, plus extra for brushing

200 g/7 oz. buffalo mozzarella (*mozzarella di bufala*) or cow's milk mozzarella (*fior di latte*)

5 ripe tomatoes, cubed

3 tablespoons chopped fresh basil

4 tablespoons freshly grated Parmesan

sea salt and freshly ground black pepper

2 large, heavy baking sheets

2 rimless baking sheets

non-stick baking parchment

Makes 4 calzone

Put the large, heavy baking sheets into the oven. Preheat the oven to 200°C (400°F) Gas 6.

Uncover the dough, punch out the air and divide into 4 balls. Dredge with flour and leave to rise on a sheet of floured baking parchment for about 20 minutes, until soft and puffy.

Meanwhile, toss the aubergine/eggplant and garlic cloves with the olive oil in a roasting pan and roast for 20 minutes. Lightly squeeze any excess moisture out of the mozzarella then cut it into cubes. Remove the roasting pan from the oven and cool for 10 minutes before stirring in the tomatoes, mozzarella and basil. Season to taste.

Roll or pull the risen balls of dough into 20-cm/8-inch circles directly onto 2 sheets of baking parchment. Slide these onto the rimless baking sheets. Spread a quarter of the vegetable mixture on one half of each calzone, leaving just over 1 cm/½ inch around the edge for sealing. Season well. Fold the uncovered half of the dough over the filling. Pinch and twist the edges firmly together so that the filling doesn't escape during cooking. Brush with olive oil and sprinkle with Parmesan.

Working quickly, open the oven door and slide both paper and calzone onto the hot baking sheets. Bake for 30 minutes (swapping the baking sheets around halfway) or until the crust is puffed up and golden. Remove from the oven and leave to cool for 2–3 minutes before serving. Serve hot or warm.

Rosemary focaccia

Focaccia al rosmarino

Focaccia literally means 'a bread that was baked on the hearth', but it is easy to bake in conventional ovens. It is found in many different forms, and can be thin and crisp, thick and soft, round or square. I make this one in a tin/pan, but it can be shaped on a baking sheet to any shape you want. The secret of a truly light focaccia lies in three risings, and dimpling the dough with your fingers so it traps olive oil while it bakes. Serve with olive oil and balsamic vinegar for dipping and a handful of good olives.

750 g/6 cups Italian '00' flour or plain/all-purpose white flour, plus extra for kneading

½ teaspoon fine sea salt

25 g/1 oz. compressed fresh yeast, 1½ tablespoons active dried yeast or 2 x 7-g/¼-oz. sachet/package fast action dried yeast

150 ml/⅔ cup good olive oil

450 ml/1¾ cups hand-hot water

coarse sea or crystal salt

sprigs of rosemary

2 shallow cake tins/pans, pie or pizza plates, 25 cm/10 inches diameter, lightly oiled

a water spray

Makes 2 deep focacce

Sift the flour and salt into a large bowl and make a well in the centre. Crumble in the fresh yeast. Pour in 3 tablespoons of the olive oil, then rub in the yeast until the mixture resembles fine breadcrumbs. Pour in the hot water and mix with your hands until the dough comes together. For other yeasts, use according to the package instructions.

Transfer the dough to a floured surface, wash and dry your hands and knead for 10 minutes until smooth and elastic. The dough should be quite soft, but if too soft to handle, knead in more flour, 1 tablespoon at a time. Put the dough in a clean, oiled bowl, cover with a damp kitchen towel and let rise in a warm place for about 30 minutes–1½ hours, until doubled in size.

Punch down the dough and cut in half. Put on a floured surface and shape each half into a round ball. Roll out into 2 circles, each 25 cm/10 inches diameter, and put in the tins/pans. Cover with a damp kitchen towel and let rise for another 30 minutes.

Remove the kitchen towel and, using your finger tips, make dimples all over the surface of the dough. They can be quite deep. Pour over the remaining oil and sprinkle generously with salt. Cover again and let rise for 30 minutes. Preheat the oven to 200°C (400°F) Gas 6. Spray the focaccia with water, sprinkle the rosemary on top and bake in the preheated oven for 20–25 minutes. Transfer to a wire rack to cool. Serve as bread with a meal, or as a snack with oil, balsamic vinegar and olives.

Parmesan soda bread

Torta reggiano

This is an unyeasted bread from Umbria that is very quick to rustle up. Little packages of baking powder are especially made for instant savoury doughs in Italy. When making this type of bread, work quickly, because as soon as the liquid comes into contact with the baking powder, a chemical reaction starts to aerate the bread. Use a light hand and get the dough into the preheated oven as soon as possible.

300 g/2⅓ cups Italian '00' flour or plain/all-purpose white flour

1 teaspoon baking powder

1 teaspoon sea salt

50 g/½ cup freshly grated Parmesan, plus extra for dusting

50 g/3½ tablespoons butter, melted and cooled

125–150 ml/½–⅔ cup milk

2 medium eggs

a 'testo', terracotta bakestone or large, heavy baking sheet

a rimless baking sheet, lined with non-stick baking parchment

Makes 1 round loaf

Put the testo, terracotta bakestone or large, heavy baking sheet on the lower shelf of the oven. Preheat the oven to 190°C (375°F) Gas 5 for at least 30 minutes.

Sift the flour, baking powder and salt into a medium mixing bowl. Stir in the Parmesan and make a well in the centre.

Whisk the cooled, melted butter with 125 ml/½ cup of the milk and the eggs, and pour into the well. Mix until just combined – overmixing will make the bread tough. The dough should be quite soft; if it isn't, add a little more milk. Turn out onto a floured work surface and knead briefly. Put the ball of dough directly onto the lined baking sheet. Pat into a disc 3 cm/1¼ inches thick. Brush with a little extra milk, then mark into wedges with the back of a knife and dust with extra Parmesan.

Working quickly, open the oven door and slide both paper and bread onto the hot testo, bakestone or baking sheet. If you are brave, try to shoot the bread into the oven so that it leaves the paper behind – this takes practice!

Bake for 15 minutes, then carefully slide out the paper. Bake for a further 5 minutes, until the crust is really golden. Remove from the oven and wrap in a clean kitchen towel. Serve warm, broken into wedges, ready to split and butter.

Meat and poultry

Braised lamb cutlets with onions, herbs and olives Costolette di agnello con cipolle e olive

A magnificent way to cook lamb long and slowly, especially if it is not as young as it might be. Liver is often served with onions cooked to melting sweetness, and this is a similar technique. The black olives enrich the dish and give it a smoky taste. The cutlets can be finished off in a medium hot oven instead of cooking on top. They are very good reheated.

8–12 lamb cutlets or chops, depending on size

100 ml/scant ½ cup olive oil

1 kg./2 lbs. onions, thinly sliced

2 tablespoons chopped fresh rosemary needles and oregano

4 anchovy fillets in oil, drained, rinsed and chopped

15 black olives, pitted

sea salt and freshly ground black pepper

rosemary sprigs, to serve

Serves 4

Season the meat on both sides with salt and pepper.

Heat half the oil in a large frying pan/skillet until very hot, then add the cutlets and quickly brown on both sides. Remove to a plate and let cool.

Heat the remaining oil in the same pan and add the onions. Cook over gentle heat for 15 minutes, stirring occasionally, until the onions begin to soften – do not let them brown. Stir in the herbs, anchovies and olives and season with salt and pepper.

Arrange the cutlets on top of the bed of onions and cover with a lid. Cook over very low heat for 20 minutes, watching that the onions don't catch and burn. Serve topped with rosemary sprigs.

Beefsteak with rocket

Tagliata con la rucola

*Italians love meat cooked very rare: you will often see a slip of a girl tucking into
a steak that would comfortably feed two – and she will eat it all. The steaks are
produced from the huge, handsome, white Chianina cattle, native to Tuscany.*

4 T-bone steaks (about 200 g/
   7 oz. each)

2 tablespoons olive oil

200 g/7 oz. wild rocket/arugula

sea salt and freshly ground
   black pepper

chopped fresh flat-leaf parsley,
   to serve

Serves 4

Brush the steaks with olive oil and season very well with salt and pepper.
Heat a griddle/ridged stovetop grill pan or light a barbecue. When the pan is
smoking hot, add the steaks and cook for 2 minutes on each side to seal, then
lower the heat and continue to cook for about 4 minutes on each side for
medium-rare steaks, less for rare.

   Transfer the steaks to a cutting board, cut the meat from the bone, and
slice it thickly. Put a pile of rocket/arugula on 4 warmed plates and arrange
the sliced meat on top. Pour any juices from the steaks onto the meat and
serve immediately, topped with a sprinkling of chopped parsley.

Pork loin roasted with rosemary and garlic Arista alla fiorentina

Redolent of early morning Italian markets where porchetta (whole pigs roasted overnight in wood-fired ovens) is sold sliced and crammed into huge bread rolls as a morning snack, this dish recreates all those tastes and smells in your oven at home. Use as much rosemary as you can so the sweet pork flesh will be suffused with its pungent aroma. Tuscans cook this on the bone and slice into thick 'chops' when cooked – I think this is a more elegant way to cook it.

1.8 kg/4 lbs. loin of pork on the bone

4 large garlic cloves

4 tablespoons chopped fresh rosemary needles

a bunch of rosemary sprigs

extra virgin olive oil, for rubbing and sautéing

300 ml/scant 1¼ cups dry white wine

sea salt and freshly ground black pepper

fine kitchen string/twine

Serves 6

Ask the butcher to bone the loin, but to give you the bones. Also ask him to remove the skin and score it to make the crackling. Turn the loin fat side down. Make deep slits all over the meat, especially in the thick part. Make a paste of the garlic, chopped rosemary, at least 1 teaspoon of salt and pepper (more will give a truly authentic flavour) in a food processor. Push this paste into all the slits in the meat and spread the remainder over the surface of the meat. Roll up and tie with fine string, incorporating some long sprigs of rosemary along its length. Weigh the meat and calculate the cooking time, allowing 25 minutes for every 500 g/1 lb. At this stage you can wrap it and leave it in the refrigerator for several hours to deepen the flavour.

When ready to cook, heat 2 tablespoons olive oil in a frying pan/skillet, unwrap the pork and brown all over. Set in a roasting pan and pour the wine over the pork. Tuck in the remaining rosemary sprigs. Place the bones in another roasting pan convex side up. Rub the pork skin with a little oil and salt. Drape the skin over the pork bones. Place the pan of crackling on the top shelf of a preheated oven, and the pork on the bottom to middle shelf. Roast at 230°C (450°F) Gas 8 for 20 minutes then reduce the heat to 200°C (400°F) Gas 6, and roast for the remaining calculated time, basting the pork loin every 20 minutes.

When cooked, rest the pork in a warm place for 15 minutes before carving into thick slices. Serve with shards of crunchy crackling and the pan juices – there is no better gravy!

Meatballs (polpette) in tomato sauce are so much part of Italian food culture that they just had to be included in this book. These are bursting with flavour from fennel seeds and garlic. When cooked, it is common practice to serve the tomato sauce with pasta as a first course, followed by the meatballs and maybe a vegetable side dish. If you make the polpette very small, you can serve them in the sauce piled on top of spaghetti. The meat mixture can also be cooked as a 'polpettone' – it is rolled into one large piece, and simmered for a couple of hours. In this case, the sauce is certainly used to dress pasta first and the meat is then sliced and served as a separate course.

Pork and fennel meatballs in tomato sauce

Polpette al finocchio in ragù

450 g/1 lb. shoulder or leg of pork

225 g/8 oz. piece of unsmoked ham or gammon

225 g/8 oz. pork belly or boneless pork chops with fat

2 garlic cloves, crushed

2 tablespoons fennel seeds

a large pinch of dried chilli/hot pepper flakes

1 tablespoon sugar

2 teaspoons sea salt

2 tablespoons crushed black peppercorns

olive oil, for sautéing (see method)

150 ml/⅔ cup dry white wine

400-g/14-oz. can chopped tomatoes

200 ml/generous ¾ cup passata (Italian strained tomatoes)

sea salt and freshly ground black pepper

electric mincer/grinder (optional)

Serves 6

Trim the shoulder of pork, ham and pork belly of any skin or connective tissue. Cut the meat into large chunks, then pass them through the coarse blade of an electric mincer/grinder or chop very finely using a large sharp knife or cleaver (do not use a food processor).

Put the meat in a large bowl, add the garlic, fennel seeds, chilli/hot pepper flakes, sugar, salt and pepper. Mix with clean hands or a large wooden spoon. At this stage, the sausage meat is ready to use, but you can cover the bowl and let it mature in the refrigerator overnight.

With dampened hands, shape into meatballs about the size of a walnut. To cook, heat 2 tablespoons of the oil in a frying pan/skillet and quickly brown the meatballs all over, in batches if necessary. Remove to a plate with a slotted spoon and add the wine. Deglaze the pan and let the wine bubble until there is only 1 tablespoon left. Add the canned tomatoes and passata and season with salt and pepper. Bring back to the boil, return the meatballs to the sauce, part-cover with a lid and simmer for 30–40 minutes, topping up with water if the sauce is becoming too dry. Serve as desired.

The Tuscans have a reputation for being great game hunters. In the past, when they used to cook little gamebirds, or 'uccelletti', they would generally season them with sage. Although this dish contains no birds, it is cooked in the same way – the sausages take the place of the birds. This is the most famous of the hundreds of ways to cook beans and is equally delicious served with roast pork – or even a homemade hamburger.

Sausages with tomato and sage bean stew

Salsicce con fagioli all'uccelletto

500 g/1 lb. dried cannellini or haricot beans or, 1 kg/2 lbs. fresh cannellini or borlotti beans, if available

a pinch of bicarbonate of soda/baking soda

8 fat fresh Italian sausages, or good butcher's sausages

85 ml/⅓ cup olive oil, plus extra for brushing

3 garlic cloves, crushed

about 10 fresh sage leaves

350 g/12 oz. fresh ripe tomatoes, skinned, deseeded and puréed, or 300 ml/scant 1¼ cups passata (Italian strained tomatoes)

sea salt and freshly ground black pepper

Serves 4

If using dried beans, cover with plenty of cold water and soak overnight. The next day, drain and rinse them, then cook in plenty of boiling water without any salt, but with a pinch of bicarbonate of soda/baking soda (to keep the skins soft) for about 1–1½ hours, until tender. Drain. If using fresh beans, shell and boil in lightly salted water for 25–30 minutes, until ready, then drain.

Brush the sausages with oil and cook under a preheated grill/broiler or over a barbecue for 15 minutes, until tender and crisp on the outside.

Meanwhile, heat the oil in a saucepan and add the garlic, sage and a few grinds of pepper. Sauté until the garlic is golden and the sage beginning to become transparent and crisp. Remove and reserve a few leaves to serve.

Add the puréed tomatoes, heat to simmering, then add the cooked beans. Cook for 10 minutes, then taste and adjust the seasoning with salt and pepper. Serve the sausages with the beans and garnished with the reserved sage leaves.

Chicken and small game birds are very popular cooked this way. They are 'spatchcocked' – that is split open and flattened, so they cook evenly. Many trattorie cook 'alla brace' – over hot coals in the hearth. To make the charcoal, a wood fire is lit, and when the wood has turned to glowing red ashes, they are spread out in an even layer and left until white on top. A low iron grill on legs is placed over the top and the spatchcocked birds sizzle over the coals. Why 'alla diavola'? The cooked chicken is said to resemble the shape of the devil's face and the chilli pepper makes it hotter than hell! The best way to eat this is definitely with your fingers.

Devilled grilled chicken Pollo alla diavola

1 chicken, about 1.5 kg/3 lbs.

200 ml/¾ cup olive oil

freshly squeezed juice of 1 lemon

2 garlic cloves, crushed

1 teaspoon dried chilli/hot pepper flakes

sea salt and freshly ground black pepper

lemon wedges, to serve

a metal mesh grill basket

Serves 4

Turn the chicken breast side down. You will see the backbone underneath the skin, finishing with the parson's nose. Take a pair of kitchen scissors and cut along one side of the backbone. Cut along the other side and you will have removed the backbone completely. Turn the bird over, breast side up and open out. Press down hard on the breastbone with the flat of your hand until you hear a crack and the bird flattens out.

Put the olive oil in a bowl, add the lemon juice, garlic, chilli/hot pepper flakes, a good pinch of salt and lots of pepper. Mix well. Pour the mixture into a shallow dish, add the chicken and turn in the marinade to coat. Cover and let marinate in the refrigerator for at least 1 hour, or overnight.

Remove the chicken from the marinade and set it flat on one side of a mesh grill basket. Clamp the basket shut. Grill or barbecue bone side first for 20 minutes. Turn it over, lower the heat and cook for 20–30 minutes, until cooked through and blackened but not burnt. Baste with the marinade from time to time. Serve hot with lemon wedges.

Hunter's-style stew

Coniglio alla cacciatora

A simple way to give ordinary chicken or rabbit all the taste of the wild hills. The secret is in the reduction of the wine and the long, slow cooking. Farmed rabbits are hugely popular in Italy and come with everything attached, which really adds to the sauce. Expect this dish to have a rich sauce of tomato, herbs and perhaps mushrooms – all available to the hunter on his expeditions. The sauce is very dark and rich, so serve with very plain fare such as polenta or just a salad afterwards.

1 chicken, about 1.5 kg/3 lbs., or 1 large rabbit (liver kept), cut into 8 pieces

4 large garlic cloves, finely chopped

1 tablespoon finely chopped fresh rosemary needles

1 teaspoon sea salt

1 teaspoon cracked black pepper

25 g/1 oz. dried porcini mushrooms

750-ml/3 cups dry red wine (1 bottle)

2 sprigs of fresh rosemary

3 tablespoons olive oil

2 tablespoons balsamic vinegar

2 tablespoons sun-dried tomato paste

400-g/14-oz can chopped tomatoes

good quality chicken stock or water (see method)

sea salt and freshly ground black pepper

soft polenta, to serve (see page 58)

Serves 4

Wash and dry the chicken or rabbit pieces. Put the garlic, rosemary, salt and pepper in a bowl, mix well, then rub it into the flesh, especially the cut sides. Cover and let marinate for about 2 hours in a cool place, or longer in the refrigerator.

Soak the porcini mushrooms in warm water for at least 20 minutes. Meanwhile pour the wine into a non-reactive pan, add the rosemary sprigs and boil hard until reduced by half. Strain and cool.

Heat the oil in a large frying pan/skillet and fry the chicken or rabbit until well browned all over. Remove to a casserole dish. If using rabbit, add the reserved liver to the pan, fry until golden, then add to the casserole.

Deglaze the pan with the balsamic vinegar, then add the cooled wine, scraping up the sediment. Whisk in the sun-dried tomato paste and tomatoes and add the porcini and their soaking water. Season with salt and pepper, bring to the boil and pour over the chicken or rabbit. Add a little water or stock so the liquid just covers the meat. Bring to the boil, then cover and simmer very gently for 45 minutes–1 hour.

Lift the chicken or rabbit onto a warm serving dish. Mash the liver, if using, into the sauce and reduce, if necessary, by boiling fast to a syrupy consistency. Pour the sauce over the chicken or rabbit and serve with soft polenta.

Veal in tuna and caper sauce Vitello tonnato

This is one of the most famous dishes to come out of Piedmont, and still a favourite. It is delightful made with turkey instead of veal if you prefer. Turkey is popular in Italy, and if cooked and cooled in the poaching liquid, it will remain nice and moist. Begin preparing this dish two days before you plan to serve it.

1 kg/2 lbs. boneless veal topside or turkey breast

600 ml/2½ cups dry white wine

1 celery stalk/rib, chopped

1 carrot, chopped

1 small onion, chopped

1 bay leaf

3 cloves

Tuna mayonnaise

200-g/7-oz. can tuna steak in oil, drained

6 anchovy fillets in oil, rinsed

2 hard-boiled egg yolks

1 tablespoon salted capers, rinsed, plus extra to serve

300 ml/scant 1¼ cups olive oil

freshly squeezed juice of 1 lemon

2 teaspoons white wine vinegar

sea salt and freshly ground black pepper

To serve

1 unwaxed lemon, thinly sliced

a few sprigs of fresh flat-leaf parsley

fine kitchen string/twine

Serves 6–8

Two days before serving, put the veal or turkey in a bowl with the wine, celery, carrot, onion, bay leaf and cloves, mix well, cover and let marinate in the refrigerator for 24 hours.

Remove the meat from the marinade and tie up neatly with fine string. If using turkey, remove the skin. Put in a saucepan just large enough to hold it. Pour in the marinade, then top up with water until the meat is just covered. Cover with a lid, bring to the boil, then reduce the heat and simmer very slowly for about 1¼ hours, until cooked through. When cooked, remove from the heat and let cool in the liquid.

When cold, remove the meat from the liquid, wrap and chill the meat and strain the liquid. Chill the liquid in the refrigerator for a couple of hours to set any grease. Lift off and discard any grease and set the liquid aside.

To make the tuna mayonnaise, put the tuna, anchovies, hard-boiled egg yolks and capers in a blender or food processor and blend until smooth. With the machine running, pour in the olive oil in a thin stream until it has all been absorbed and the mixture is thick and homogenized. Scrape out into a bowl and season to taste with the lemon juice and vinegar.

Using the poaching liquid, carefully dilute the sauce until it is the right flowing consistency. Taste and adjust the seasoning with salt and pepper. Slice the veal or turkey thinly. Spread a few tablespoons of the sauce on serving plates. Add a layer of veal, coat with the sauce and continue until all is used up, ending with sauce. Sprinkle the some extra capers on top, add the slices of lemon and a few parsley sprigs and serve immediately.

Fish and seafood

Grilled sardines with salmoriglio sauce

Sarde alla griglia con salmoriglio

The smell of silvery blue sardines on a grill is unmistakable – it is one of the most appetizing scents in outdoor cooking. Sardines grill very well because they are an oily fish and are self-basting. Great shoals of them are to be found in Mediterranean waters in May and June, which is the best time to eat them. They are eaten grilled or fried, boned or stuffed, always 'con gusto'!

12 fat fresh sardines

extra virgin olive oil, plus extra for brushing

lemon wedges, to serve

Salmoriglio sauce

2 tablespoons red wine vinegar

1–2 teaspoons sugar

finely grated zest and freshly squeezed juice of ½ a lemon

4 tablespoons extra virgin olive oil

1 garlic clove, finely chopped

1 tablespoon crumbled dried oregano (not fresh)

1 tablespoon salted capers, rinsed and chopped

a barbecue grill rack

Serves 4

To make the salmoriglio sauce, put the vinegar and sugar in a bowl and stir to dissolve. Add the lemon zest and juice. Whisk in the olive oil, then add the garlic, oregano and capers. Set aside to infuse.

Using the back of a knife, scale the sardines, starting from the tail and working towards the head. Slit open the belly and remove the insides, then rinse the fish and pat dry with paper towels. Clip off any fins you don't want to see. Brush the fish with olive oil and arrange on a grill rack (there are racks especially made in a wheel shape for sardines).

Cook under a preheated grill/broiler or over a barbecue for about 3 minutes per side, until sizzling hot and charring. Serve with the salmoriglio sauce spooned over the top, with lots of lemon wedges for squeezing alongside.

Sea bass has a wonderful, clean, fresh taste and cooking in paper is the best way to cook whole fish (with the possible exception of grilling over embers). The paper lets the fish steam in its own juices, absorbing the aroma of the fresh herbs and lemon. This cooking time should be perfect – the fish is better slightly underdone at the bone than overdone. The packages should be opened at the table to appreciate the full aroma.

Sea bass baked with lemon and bay leaves

Branzino al cartoccio al limone e alloro

2 whole sea bass, about 350 g/
   12 oz. each, cleaned and scaled

about 1 tablespoon olive oil

4 fresh bay leaves

2 sprigs of fresh thyme

6 thin slices of unwaxed lemon

2 tablespoons dry white wine or
   freshly squeezed lemon juice

sea salt and freshly ground
   black pepper

non-stick baking parchment

Serves 2

Preheat the oven to 190°C (375°F) Gas 5.

Cut 2 large rectangles of baking parchment big enough to wrap each fish generously. Brush the rectangles with a little oil.

Season the cavities of the fish with salt and pepper. Put 2 bay leaves in each one and tuck in the thyme and lemon slices.

Put one fish on one half of the paper, sprinkle with white wine or lemon juice, fold over the other half loosely and twist or fold the edges tightly together to seal. Repeat with the other fish, then carefully transfer both packages to a baking sheet.

Bake in the preheated oven for 20 minutes. Put each package on a hot serving plate for each diner to open for themselves.

Tuna is a very filling and rich fish. Although one never thinks of cooking it with rosemary, it is in fact a marriage made in heaven – especially when flavoured with very good olive oil and some capers to cut the richness.

Tuna steaks baked with rosemary and capers

Tonno al cartoccio al rosmarino e capperi

4 x 150-g/5½-oz. tuna steaks

2 tablespoons chopped fresh rosemary needles, plus extra sprigs to garnish (optional)

1 tablespoon salted capers, rinsed and chopped

4 tablespoons dry white wine

4 tablespoons extra virgin olive oil

sea salt and freshly ground black pepper

lemon wedges, to serve

non-stick baking parchment

Serves 4

Preheat the oven to 180°C (350°F) Gas 4.

Cut 4 rectangles of baking parchment big enough to wrap each tuna steak generously. Brush the rectangles with a little oil.

Transfer each steak to a piece of paper. Coat with the chopped rosemary, scatter the capers over the top then pour the wine over. Season well with salt and pepper, then drizzle with olive oil.

Loosely but securely twist or close the parchment around the tuna – it should be loose enough to fill with steam as it cooks, but secure enough not to let the juices escape during the cooking. Carefully transfer the packages to a baking sheet.

Bake in the preheated oven for 15 minutes. Put each package on a hot serving plate for each diner, open and garnish with rosemary sprigs (if using). Serve with lemon wedges for squeezing.

This dish originated in Venice during the Renaissance and has been cooked and served on gondolas on the eve of the Feast of the Redeemer in July ever since. As well as adding flavour to the delicate fish, the marinade slightly preserves it too. I have eaten this simple dish beside the Venetian lagoon with a big basket of bread and a glass of crisp, throat-tingling white wine, watching the mirage of the water meeting the sky. This dish can also be made with fresh sardines, but sole is popular in Venice.

Fillets of sole in sweet and sour onion marinade Sogliole in saor

8 sole fillets, skinned

plain/all-purpose flour, for dusting

100 ml/scant ½ cup olive oil

sea salt and freshly ground
    black pepper

Onion marinade

50 ml/¼ cup olive oil

2 mild onions, finely sliced

3 fresh bay leaves (or a sprig of
    leaves if available)

100 ml/⅓ cup white wine vinegar

Serves 4

To make the onion marinade, heat the olive oil in a frying pan/skillet set over medium heat. Add the onions and bay leaves. Cook, stirring, for about 15–20 minutes, until the onions are soft and translucent and not browned at all. Add the vinegar and boil rapidly for a few minutes until amalgamated with the onion juices. Remove from the heat, pour into a bowl and set aside.

Season the sole fillets with salt, and dip them in flour to coat both sides, shaking to remove the excess.

Heat the olive oil in a frying pan/skillet and fry the sole fillets for about 1 minute on each side. Remove and drain on paper towels.

Spoon half of the cooled onion marinade into a shallow serving dish, season with pepper and arrange the sole fillets on top. Pour in the remaining marinade, cover with clingfilm/plastic wrap and let marinate for several hours or overnight in the refrigerator. Serve at room temperature.

Grilled tuna steaks with red pepper sauce

Tonno alla griglia con peperonata

Tuna is a very rich meat and is always cut thinly in Italy – never as thick as the seared steaks we are used to. Marinating the slices in mustard and grappa gives them a piquant crust – so good with the sweet peppers. Overcooking tuna can make it very dry, so watch it like a hawk.

4 tuna steaks, cut 1 cm/½ inch thick

olive oil, for cooking

Marinade

4 garlic cloves

3 tablespoons Dijon mustard

2 tablespoons grappa or brandy

sea salt and freshly ground black pepper

Peperonata

6 tablespoons olive oil

1 kg/2 lbs. fresh ripe tomatoes, skinned, deseeded and chopped, or 2 x 400-g/14-oz. cans chopped tomatoes

½ teaspoon dried chilli/hot pepper flakes

2 onions, finely sliced

3 garlic cloves, chopped

3 large red (bell) peppers, halved, deseeded and cut into thin strips

sea salt and freshly ground black pepper

Serves 4

To make the marinade, crush the garlic, put in a bowl and beat in the mustard and grappa. Season with salt and pepper and use to spread over the cut sides of the tuna. Arrange in a non-metal dish, cover and let marinate in a cool place for about 1 hour.

To make the peperonata, heat 3 tablespoons of the oil in a saucepan, then add the tomatoes and chilli/hot pepper flakes. Cook over medium heat for about 10 minutes, until the tomatoes disintegrate.

Heat the remaining oil in a frying pan/skillet, add the onions, garlic and peppers and sauté for about 10 minutes until softening. Add the pepper mixture to the tomatoes and simmer, covered with a lid, for about 45 minutes, until very soft. Season to taste with salt and pepper.

Preheat the grill/broiler or barbecue. Sprinkle the tuna steaks with olive oil and arrange on a rack over a foil-lined grill/broiler pan. Grill/broil for 2 minutes on each side, until crusty on the outside and still pink in the middle. Alternatively, barbecue over hot embers for slightly less time. Serve with the peperonata, which can be served hot or cold, as preferred.

A big fish stew — Brodetto di pesce

1 kg/2 lbs. live mussels and clams

500 g/1 lb. small squid, cleaned

8 raw prawns/shrimp (optional)

1.75 kg/4 lbs. mixed whole but cleaned fish (see Note)

Flavoured broth

150 ml/⅔ cup extra virgin olive oil

4 leeks, sliced and well washed

4 garlic cloves, finely chopped

300 ml/scant 1¼ cups dry white wine

a large pinch of saffron threads

750 g/1 lb. 10 oz. ripe plum tomatoes, coarsely chopped

2 tablespoons sun-dried tomato paste or 6 sun-dried tomatoes in oil, drained and coarsely chopped

1 teaspoon fennel seeds

1 tablespoon dried oregano

sea salt and freshly ground black pepper

To serve

chopped fresh flat-leaf parsley

lemon wedges

crusty bread

Serves 6—8

On Fridays and market days, fish is the best thing to buy. This stew is the perfect family feast and typical of many coastal trattorie. Try to include a good selection of fish. In Italy, there are boxes of fish on market stalls labelled 'per zuppa', which means small or bony fish with lots of flavour, only for soups or stews. A well-flavoured base broth is essential, including saffron and fennel seeds, and the fish is then poached in this liquid. The fish is served separately and the broth is ladled on top.

First prepare the seafood. Scrub and debeard the mussels. Tap all the mussels and clams against the work surface. Discard any that don't close – they are dead – and also any with damaged shells. Keep in a bowl of cold water until ready to cook.

To make the broth, heat the olive oil in a large, deep stockpot and add the leeks and garlic. Cook gently for about 5 minutes, until softened. Pour in the white wine and boil rapidly until reduced by half. Add the saffron, tomatoes, sun-dried tomato paste, fennel seeds and oregano. Pour in 600 ml/2½ cups water and bring to the boil. Turn down the heat, cover with a lid and simmer for 20 minutes, until the tomatoes and oil separate.

Start cooking the fish. Add the squid to the pan and poach for 3–4 minutes. Remove with a slotted spoon, put on a plate, cover and keep them warm. Add the prawns/shrimp, if using, and simmer just until opaque. Remove with a slotted spoon and keep warm with the squid. Add the mussels and clams to the broth, cover and boil for a few minutes until they open. Remove with a slotted spoon and keep them warm. Discard any that haven't opened.

Poach all the remaining fish, until just cooked. Remove from the broth, arrange in warmed soup plates and put the squid, prawns/shrimp (if using), mussels and clams on top. Taste the broth and season with salt and pepper if necessary. Ladle the broth over the fish, sprinkle with chopped parsley and serve with lemon wedges for squeezing and crusty bread.

NOTE Choose at least 4 varieties of fish – the greater the variety, the more intense the flavour. Do not choose oily fish like salmon, herring or sardines. Choose from: cod, grouper, halibut, monkfish, red gurnard, hake, John Dory, red mullet, swordfish, tilefish, rascasse, weaver, whiting or wrasse.

Salads and sides

Italian mixed salad Insalata mista

If you ask for a mixed salad in Italy, this is what you will get. Don't be surprised if the tomatoes are not red and ripe, but hard and green – this is how they are eaten in salads. If you think about it, this dish is to cleanse the palate after a meat or fish course, and that is just what it does. Leaving the skins on potatoes and tomatoes is generally not done, but you can do it at home. Salads do not come dressed – bottles of oil and vinegar are given to you so that you may dress your own. The vinegar is often red wine vinegar; balsamic vinegar is not likely to appear in a trattoria.

350 g/12 oz. waxy salad potatoes
175 g/6 oz. fine green beans
extra virgin olive oil
50 g/¼ cup pitted green olives
1 small crisp lettuce
2 large ripe tomatoes, quartered
3 tablespoons chopped fresh
    flat-leaf parsley
sea salt and freshly ground
    black pepper

To serve

a small bottle of good olive oil
a small bottle of red wine vinegar

Serves 4

Peel the potatoes and boil in salted water for about 15 minutes, until tender, adding the beans 4 minutes before the potatoes are ready. Drain and cover with cold water to stop the cooking.

When cold, drain well. Transfer the beans to a bowl, slice the potatoes thickly and add to the beans, moistening with a little olive oil. Add the olives and toss well.

Wash the lettuce and tear into bite-size pieces. Add the lettuce and tomatoes to the potatoes and beans and toss lightly. Transfer to a serving bowl, season with salt and pepper and sprinkle over the parsley.

Serve the olive oil and vinegar separately and let diners dress their own salads at the table.

In Sicily, the land of orange and lemon groves, this salad is often served after grilled fish – especially in the region around Palermo. It is another example of their passion for sweet and savoury combinations and is very refreshing.

Orange, frisée and black olive salad

Insalata di arance, indivia e olive nere

2 oranges

1 red onion

140 g/5 oz. frisée (curly endive)
  or escarole

Dressing

finely grated zest and juice of
  1 orange

6 tablespoons extra virgin olive oil

2 tablespoons finely sliced fresh
  basil leaves

2 tablespoons finely chopped,
  pitted, Greek-style, oven-dried
  black olives

2 sun-dried tomatoes in oil,
  finely chopped

sea salt and freshly ground
  black pepper

serves 4

To make the dressing, put the orange zest and juice, olive oil, basil, olives and sun-dried tomatoes in a large bowl. Mix well, season with salt and pepper and set aside to develop the flavours.

Peel the oranges with a sharp knife, removing all the skin and white pith. Cut out the segments. Set aside in a bowl. Finely slice the onion, using a very sharp thin-bladed knife or a mandolin if you have one. Immediately toss the onion and oranges in the dressing to prevent discoloration. Let marinate in a cool place for 15 minutes.

Arrange the frisée on serving plates and pile the dressed orange and onion mixture in the middle, spooning over any remaining dressing. Serve immediately.

Braised fennel with olive oil, lemon and chilli

Finocchi alla diavola

Braising fennel slowly makes it meltingly soft and tender. Here the aniseedy fennel absorbs all the flavours of the olive oil, lemon juice and chilli and the anchovy adds a salty touch. This is delicious with pork dishes and more robust fish like swordfish. This is best eaten the day after it is made when the flavours have matured.

4 heads of fennel

200 ml/¾ cup extra virgin olive oil

finely grated zest and juice of
   1 large lemon

1 anchovy in oil or salt, rinsed
   and finely chopped

½ teaspoon dried chilli/hot
   pepper flakes

a little white wine vinegar

sea salt and freshly ground
   black pepper

a flameproof baking dish

Serves 4—6

Preheat the oven to 160°C (325°F) Gas 3.

Trim the stalks and fronds from the fennel. Discard the stalks, but keep the green fronds. Halve the fennel bulbs. Cut out the hard core, then cut each half into 2 wedges. Arrange in a flameproof baking dish.

Put the olive oil, lemon zest and juice, anchovy, chilli/hot pepper flakes, vinegar, salt and pepper in a bowl and whisk well. Pour over the fennel. Bring the dish to the boil on top of the stove. Cover with kitchen foil and bake in the preheated oven for about 1 hour, until very soft and tender.

Remove from the oven and take off the foil. Taste the liquid and add a dash more vinegar to sharpen it if necessary. Serve warm or cold, sprinkled with the reserved fennel fronds.

Grilled and sautéed mushrooms

Funghi trifolati

You will often see this dish on Italian menus, and it usually means that the mushrooms are sliced and sautéed, then finished off with the reduction of wine and olive oil. This is good if the mushrooms are small, but when it is mushroom season and you have the opportunity of cooking larger mushrooms, this is the way to do it. I have also come across them being grilled over a bed of charcoal and the smell was fantastic.

4 large portobello mushrooms or
   4 fresh porcini mushrooms

olive oil (see method)

200 ml/¾ cup white wine

2 garlic cloves, chopped

freshly squeezed juice of 1 lemon

3 tablespoons chopped fresh
   flat-leaf parsley

sea salt and freshly ground
   black pepper

Serves 4

Preheat the grill/broiler.

Pull the stalks off the mushrooms and set the caps, gill side up, on an oiled grill/broiler pan. Chop the stalks finely and set aside. Brush the mushrooms with olive oil, season with salt and pepper and cook under the preheated grill/broiler for 5 minutes.

Meanwhile, put 3 tablespoons olive oil in a frying pan/skillet with the white wine, garlic, lemon juice, parsley and the reserved chopped stalks. Bring to the boil, then boil hard to reduce by half. Season well and take off the heat. Transfer the mushrooms to warm serving plates and pour the sauce over the top. Serve immediately.

Spinach with eggs and cream Spinaci con uove

This is my version of a famous Florentine dish of spinach and béchamel sauce baked with eggs. Although it is delicious, I think you can taste the spinach and fresh farm eggs much better when cooked with cream instead of the sauce. A good grating of nutmeg is essential here, and plenty of salt and pepper.

1 kg/2 lbs. fresh spinach

50 g/3 tablespoons butter

250 ml/1 cup single/light cream

4 very fresh eggs

freshly grated nutmeg

3 tablespoons freshly grated
Parmesan

sea salt and freshly ground
black pepper

a baking dish, buttered

Serves 4

Preheat the oven to 200°C (400°F) Gas 6.

Pull the stalks off the spinach leaves and discard them. Wash the leaves very well in plenty of cold water, then chop roughly. Melt the butter in a large saucepan, add the spinach and cook until wilted. Lift out the spinach and drain through a colander, catching any juices that run out.

Arrange the spinach in the prepared baking dish. Carefully pour over the cream, then make 4 indentations in the spinach and crack an egg in each one. Pour the collected spinach juices back into the pan and boil to reduce. Season with salt, pepper and nutmeg and pour over the cream and spinach. Sprinkle with the Parmesan and bake in the preheated oven for 15–20 minutes, until the eggs have set and the whole dish is bubbling. Serve immediately.

Peas with prosciutto Piselli al prosciutto

Fresh peas need almost no cooking at all, and this dish makes the most of their freshness. If I have time, I like to make use of the pea pods which are bursting with flavour, so I make a quick pea stock to give the dish extra flavour. Add more stock if the dish looks dry – there should be plenty of sweet, buttery juices. This is also a good way with frozen peas, which are after all peas picked in their prime and fast frozen.

1 kg/2 lbs. fresh peas in their pods
(to give about 500 g/1 lb.
podded weight)

150 g/6 oz. Italian dry-cured ham,
such as *prosciutto crudo* or a
smoked bacon such as *pancetta*

50 g/3 tablespoons butter

1 small onion, finely chopped

sea salt and freshly ground
black pepper

Serves 4

Shell the peas, reserving the pods and peas separately. Roughly chop the pods, put them into a saucepan, barely cover with water and bring to the boil. Simmer for 10 minutes, strain and set aside.

Slice the prosciutto into thin strips or cube the pancetta. Melt the butter in a medium saucepan, add the onion and cook gently for 5 minutes until softening but not colouring. Add the fresh peas and 100 ml/scant ½ cup pea stock and salt and pepper to taste. Stir well, cover and simmer for 5 minutes. Uncover, add the prosciutto or pancetta and stir it in. Cook over a moderate heat for a few minutes then serve immediately.

Baked aubergine, tomato, mozzarella and parmesan Parmigiana di melanzane

My friend Louise, who lives in Italy, goes completely crazy for this dish. She always persuades me to put it on the menu for my guests on our cooking course in Tuscany, but it's really for her. It is very rich and deserves to be eaten on its own. It is said to originate in Campania and is often confused with melanzane alla Parmigiana, which is another dish altogether. Sometimes it is layered with hard-boiled eggs, but I like it better without. This is easily prepared in advance and refrigerated to put in the oven at a moment's notice.

4 aubergines/eggplants

2 tablespoons olive oil, plus extra for the aubergines/eggplants

1 small onion, finely chopped

2 x 400-g/14-oz. cans chopped tomatoes, drained

2 tablespoons chopped fresh basil

50–75 g/½–¾ cup freshly grated Parmesan

200 g/7 oz. mozzarella cheese, thinly sliced

sea salt and freshly ground black pepper

a shallow baking dish, lightly oiled

Serves 4

Cut the aubergines/eggplants lengthwise into strips 1 cm/½ inch wide. Soak them for 30 minutes in a bowl of salted water.

Heat the oil in a frying pan/skillet, add the onion and cook for 5 minutes until softening, then add the tomatoes and basil and simmer gently for about 30 minutes. Season with salt and pepper.

Drain the aubergines/eggplants, then rinse and pat dry with paper towels. Shallow fry them or brush with olive oil and roast in a preheated oven at 180°C (350°F) Gas 4 for about 20 minutes until deep golden brown. Set aside. If the oven isn't already on, preheat it to 180°C (350°F) Gas 4.

Arrange the aubergines/eggplants in a single layer in the prepared baking dish, then add a layer of grated Parmesan, followed by a layer of mozzarella slices and a layer of the tomato sauce. Continue layering in this order until all the ingredients are used up, ending with a sauce layer (this will keep the dish moist – if you want a crisp top, end with aubergine/eggplant and Parmesan).

Bake in the preheated oven for 30–35 minutes, until browned and bubbling. Remove from the oven and let sit for 10 minutes to settle before serving. Serve warm or at room temperature.

Pumpkin roasted with sage and onion

Zucca arrostita con cipolle e salvia

Pumpkin is a popular vegetable throughout Italy, and is generally made into soup or used to fill ravioli. However, if the flesh is not too watery, it is delicious roasted in olive oil on a bed of fresh sage and sliced onions.

750 g/1 lb. 10 oz. fresh pumpkin or butternut squash

6 tablespoons extra virgin olive oil

2 large onions, sliced

12 fresh sage leaves

a pinch of dried chilli/hot pepper flakes

1 tablespoon balsamic vinegar

sea salt and freshly ground black pepper

a metal or enamel roasting pan

Serves 4

Preheat the oven to 220°C (425°F) Gas 7.

Scoop the seeds out of the pumpkin and cut away the skin. Cut into long slices or chunks. Pour 4 tablespoons olive oil into a roasting pan and add the onion. Season with salt and pepper and toss well to coat. Scatter the pumpkin over the onion and the sage leaves over the pumpkin. Drizzle with the remaining olive oil, scatter over the chilli/hot pepper flakes and season well with salt and pepper.

Roast in the preheated oven for 25–30 minutes, until tender and beginning to brown. Sprinkle with the vinegar while it is still hot, then serve.

Roasted tomatoes with a secret Pomodori al forno

Plum tomatoes are perfect for roasting as they have a low moisture content, have less tendency to burst and remain quite meaty. This recipe, along with plain boiled green beans tossed in olive oil, is one of the most popular side dishes in Italian trattorie. A whole garlic clove is buried in the middle of each tomato, which perfumes the entire tomato and softens to a silky texture.

6 large ripe plum or round tomatoes, with their stalks on if possible

6 small garlic cloves, peeled

extra virgin olive oil, for drizzling

sea salt and freshly ground black pepper

a baking dish, lightly oiled

Serves 6

Preheat the oven to 160°C (325°F) Gas 3.

Cut a thin sliver off the base of each tomato so it will stand upright. Cut off the tops and push a garlic clove deep inside each tomato. Season with salt and pepper and replace the tops.

Arrange the tomatoes in the prepared baking dish. They should be upright and close together. Drizzle with olive oil and season again with salt and pepper. Bake in the preheated oven for about 2 hours, checking every now and then. They should be slightly shrivelled, and a brilliant red. Take them out and insert a sharp knife in the middle to see if the garlic clove is soft – it must be very soft. Replace the tops and serve hot or cold, as preferred.

Sweet things

Spiced cookies with candied orange and walnuts Cavallucci

These crunchy cookies are a speciality from Siena and at one time probably had the image of a horse stamped on the surface, in the tradition of the Palio (Siena horse race). They keep well in an airtight container.

200 g/1 cup caster/superfine sugar
6 tablespoons clear honey
200 g/1½ generous cups walnut pieces, chopped
85 g/3 oz. candied orange peel, finely diced
½ teaspoon ground aniseed
½ teaspoon ground cinnamon
¼ teaspoon ground cloves
500 g/4 cups plain/all-purpose white flour
1 tablespoon baking powder
icing/confectioners' sugar, for dusting

a baking sheet, floured

Makes 16

Put the sugar and honey in a saucepan with 200 ml/¾ cup water. Stir and heat gently until dissolved, then boil to the 'thread' stage. Remove from the heat and stir in the walnuts and orange peel.

Preheat the oven to 180°C (350°F) Gas 4. Sift the flour with the baking powder and spices in a bowl, then pour in the walnut and orange peel mixture and fold into the flour. Tip out and knead the dough – it should be quite firm. Divide into 16 pieces and roll into rough balls, whilst still warm. Put on the prepared baking sheet and bake in the preheated oven for about 20–25 minutes, until puffed and set but not browned. Dust with icing/confectioners' sugar just before serving.

Soft almond cookies

Ricciarelli

These delicate cookies, also from Siena, are said to resemble the almond-shaped eyes of the Madonna in Renaissance paintings. They are associated with the Feast of the Annunciation and, consequently, with fertility. Use whole blanched almonds, if you can, as they are fresher this way.

175 g/2 cups whole blanched almonds, ground, or 175 g/1¾ cups ground almonds
200 g/1 cup caster/superfine sugar, plus extra for rolling
½ teaspoon baking powder
1 tablespoon plain/all-purpose white flour
2 large egg whites
3 drops almond extract
icing/confectioners' sugar, to serve

a baking sheet, lined with baking parchment

Makes 16

Put the almonds in a bowl with the sugar. Sift the baking powder with the flour into the almonds and sugar. Whisk the egg whites until stiff but not dry, then stir into the almond mixture. Add the almond extract and blend until you have a soft malleable paste.

Preheat the oven to 200°C (400°F) Gas 6. Pour some caster/superfine sugar onto a plate. Roll heaped tablespoons of the mixture into small balls, roll in the sugar, and then press into the traditional oval shape by rolling into a fat sausage, tapering the ends, then flattening slightly with the palm of your hand. Put the cookies on the prepared baking sheet. Bake in the preheated oven for 10–12 minutes, until lightly golden. Transfer to a wire rack to cool. Press the tops into icing/confectioners' sugar before serving.

Panna cotta with candied orange zest

The secret of a great panna cotta is in the wobble. I have eaten many indifferent versions – some of them made from packet mixes. This one is really good. Panna cotta means 'cooked or scalded cream' and is said to have originated in Piedmont or Lombardy, where the cream and milk are very rich.

500 ml/2 cups double/heavy cream

300 ml/scant 1¼ cups milk

1 vanilla bean, split

50 g/¼ cup caster/superfine sugar

3 leaves of gelatine/gelatin or 3 teaspoons powdered gelatine/gelatin (see Note)

Candied orange zest

2 unwaxed oranges

50 g/¼ cup caster/superfine sugar

6 moulds/molds, each about 125 ml/½ cup capacity

Serves 6

Put the cream and milk, split vanilla bean and sugar in a saucepan and bring to the boil. Crumble or sprinkle the gelatine into the cream and stir until dissolved. Cool, then chill in the refrigerator until it JUST begins to thicken. At this stage, stir the cream briskly to distribute the vanilla seeds, then remove the vanilla bean. Pour into the moulds, set on a tray and chill for at least 5 hours, until set.

Remove the zest from the oranges with a sharp potato peeler (removing any bitter white pith with a knife afterwards). Cut the zest into long, fine shreds. Bring a small saucepan of water to the boil and blanch the shreds for 1 minute. Drain, then refresh in cold water. Put the sugar and 100 ml/scant ½ cup water in a separate small saucepan and stir until dissolved. Add the orange shreds and bring to a rolling boil. Boil for 2–3 minutes, then strain through a sieve/strainer, reserving the syrup, and transfer the shreds to a plate to cool. Before they cool too much, separate them out a little.

To serve, press the top of each panna cotta and gently pull away from the edge of the mould. Carefully invert onto a small cold plate. (Give the mould a good shake and the panna cotta should drop out.) If it still won't turn out, dip very briefly into warm water, then invert onto the plate again and lift off. Top with the candied orange zest and a spoonful of the reserved syrup.

NOTE: Panna cotta must be wobbly. However, if you are nervous about turning them out, use 4 sheets gelatine/gelatin instead of 3. The panna cotta will melt if the dipping water is too hot.

Lemon sorbet

Sorbetto al limone

It's worth making a journey to Italy just to taste lemons that have been properly ripened in the sun. Walk through a lemon grove when the glossy green trees are in blossom and the scent is intoxicating. The beautiful leaves can be used like bay leaves or the more exotic Thai lime leaves to impart a lemony flavour to sweet and savoury dishes alike. I mix the orange with the lemon juice in this recipe, because it softens the acidity of our un-sunkissed lemons.

300 g/1½ cups caster/superfine sugar

finely grated zest and freshly squeezed juice of 6 lemons, plus 6 even-sized lemons, to serve

finely grated zest and juice of 1 orange

an ice cream maker (optional)

Serves 6

Put the sugar and 600 ml/2½ cups water in a saucepan with the lemon and orange zest. Bring slowly to the boil and boil rapidly for 3–4 minutes. Remove from the heat, and let cool. Meanwhile, strain the fruit juices into a bowl. When the syrup is cold, strain into the bowl of juice. Chill. When cold, churn in an ice cream maker.

Alternatively, pour into a shallow freezer tray and freeze until is frozen around the edges. Mash well with a fork. When it is half-frozen again, blend in a food processor until creamy, then cover and freeze until firm.

Meanwhile, cut the tops off the remaining 6 lemons and shave a little off each base so that it will stand up. Scoop out the insides, squeeze and keep the juice for another time. Put in the freezer. When the sorbet is frozen use it to fill the lemon shells then set the tops back on. Return to the freezer until needed. Soften in the refrigerator for 10–15 minutes before serving.

Vanilla gelato with hot cherry sauce

Gelato alla vaniglia con amarene

At last, an ice cream that actually tastes like a real Italian gelato. There is no cream and no eggs, so no custard making. It is silky smooth and heavenly, served in a glass dish or 'coppa' with delicious warmed Amarena cherries. Amarena cherries are sold in pretty white and blue glass jars – a great souvenir of a holiday in Italy – but are less expensive bought in cans from the deli counter of your local Italian grocer.

1 vanilla bean

1.125 litres/4½ cups full cream milk

2 tablespoons dried skimmed milk powder/non-fat dry milk

4 tablespoons cornflour/cornstarch or wheat starch

275 g/1⅓ cups caster/superfine sugar

1 teaspoon real vanilla extract

375-g/13-oz. can Italian Amarena cherries in syrup

2 tablespoons maraschino liqueur or kirsch

an ice cream maker (optional)

Serves 6

Split the vanilla bean in two and put in a saucepan with 900 ml/3½ cups of the milk. Whisk in the milk powder/dry milk. Bring to boiling point, turn off the heat and leave to infuse for 20 minutes.

Remove the vanilla bean and scrape out the seeds into the milk. Whisk the seeds through the milk.

Dissolve the cornflour/cornstarch in the remaining milk, then pour into the hot milk and add the sugar. Set over the heat again and bring to the boil, stirring constantly until thickened. Cover the surface with clingfilm/plastic wrap and let cool to room temperature. Stir in the vanilla extract. Chill, then churn in an ice cream maker.

Alternatively, pour into a shallow freezer tray and freeze until it is frozen around the edges. Mash well with a fork. When it is half-frozen again, blend in a food processor until creamy, then cover and freeze until firm. Let soften in the refrigerator for 20 minutes before serving.

When ready to serve, put the cherries, their syrup and the liqueur in a saucepan and heat gently. Serve the ice cream in large scoops with the sauce trickled over it.

Zabaglione

There is nothing quite as sensual as warm zabaglione served straight from the pan. Many like to beat it in a copper bowl so that it cooks quickly. The secret is not to let the mixture get too hot, but still hot enough to cook and thicken the egg yolks. The proportions are easy to remember: one egg yolk to one tablespoon sugar to one tablespoon Marsala, serves one person. It must be made at the last moment, but it doesn't take long and is well worth the effort.

2 large egg yolks

2 tablespoons sweet Marsala wine

2 tablespoons caster/superfine
 sugar

about 6 sponge fingers/lady fingers
 (Italian *savoiardi* cookies),
 to serve

Serves 2

Put the egg yolks, Marsala and sugar in a medium heatproof bowl (preferably copper or stainless steel) and beat with a hand-held electric mixer or a balloon whisk until well blended.

Set the bowl over a saucepan of gently simmering water – the bottom should at no time be in contact with the water. Do not let the water boil. Whisk the mixture until it is glossy, pale, light and fluffy and holds a trail when dropped from the whisk. This should take about 5 minutes. Serve immediately in warmed cocktail glasses with sponge fingers for dipping.

VARIATION To make chilled zabaglione for 2, when cooked, remove the bowl from the heat and whisk until completely cold. In a separate bowl, whisk 150 ml/⅔ cup double/heavy cream until floppy, then fold into the cold zabaglione. Spoon into glasses and chill for 2–3 hours before serving.

Lemon and almond tart

Torta di limone e mandorle

A refreshing change from the classic French tarte au citron. The almonds give the tart more body and add another flavour dimension. Traditionally, this is made with freshly ground almonds, because they have a fine, creamy texture and a better flavour than the ready-ground kind, which are difficult to find in Italy. If you'd like to try this method, grind the same weight of whole blanched almonds with half the sugar to prevent them becoming oily. Beat the eggs with the remaining sugar then stir in the ground sugar and almonds.

Shortcrust pastry

200 g/2 sticks unsalted butter

300 g/2 cups plain/all-purpose
   flour

100 g/½ cup caster/superfine sugar

2 egg yolks

Lemon and almond filling

4 large eggs, lightly beaten

120 g/⅔ cup caster/superfine sugar

finely grated zest and freshly
   squeezed juice of 3 lemons

120 g/1 stick unsalted butter,
   melted

120 g/scant ⅔ cup ground almonds

whipped cream, to serve

*a fluted tart tin/pan, 23 cm/
   9 inches diameter*

kitchen foil and baking beans

Serves 8

To make the pastry, work the butter into the flour and sugar until it looks like grated Parmesan.

Put the 2 egg yolks in a small bowl, add 1 tablespoon water and beat lightly. Add to the flour mixture and knead lightly until smooth. Knead into a ball, flatten, then wrap in clingfilm/plastic wrap and let it rest for about 30 minutes.

Preheat the oven to 190°C (375°F) Gas 5. Roll out the pastry on a floured surface and use to line the tart tin/pan. Prick the base all over with a fork, then chill or freeze for 15 minutes to set the pastry. Line with foil, flicking the edges inwards towards the centre so that it doesn't catch on the pastry. Fill with baking beans, set on a baking sheet and bake blind in the centre of the preheated oven for 10–12 minutes.

Remove the foil and beans and return the pastry case to the oven for a further 5–7 minutes to dry out completely.

To make the filling, put the eggs, sugar, lemon zest and juice in a bowl and whisk until light and fluffy. Stir in the melted butter and almonds. Mix well and pour into the prepared pastry case. Bake in the preheated oven for about 25–30 minutes, until the crust and the top of the tart is golden brown. Cool, then chill before serving with whipped cream.

Caramelized fig tart

Crostata di fichi

You'll find simple tarts made with seasonal fruit all over Italy. Unless the trattoria has a talented baker behind the scenes, tarts will be bought in from a local pasticceria. The ricotta makes a lovely light cheesecake with a slightly grainy texture. Be sure to try this only with fresh figs – dried are not the same. If figs aren't in season, all sorts of other fruits can be used to top the tart, such as plums.

90 g/6 tablespoons unsalted butter, softened

6 tablespoons sugar

3 egg yolks

½ teaspoon real vanilla extract

175 g/1 cup plain/all-purpose flour, plus extra for dusting

1 teaspoon sea salt

1 egg yolk, beaten, for brushing

Fig filling

225 g/8 oz. fresh ricotta

125 g/1 stick plus 1 tablespoon butter, softened

125 g/⅔ cup caster/superfine sugar

2 eggs

8–10 ripe black figs (depending on size), cut in halves or quarters

redcurrant or raspberry jelly

parchment paper

a loose-bottomed tart tin/pan, 20 cm/8 inches diameter

kitchen foil and baking beans

a baking sheet

Serves 6

To make the pastry, put the butter, sugar, the 3 egg yolks and vanilla extract in a food processor and blend until smooth.

Sift the flour and salt onto a sheet of parchment paper. Shoot the flour into the food processor and blend until just mixed.

Transfer to a floured work surface and knead gently until smooth. Form into a ball, flatten and wrap in clingfilm/plastic wrap. Chill in the refrigerator for at least 30 minutes.

To make the filling, put the ricotta, butter and sugar in a bowl and beat until smooth. Put the 2 eggs in another bowl, beat well, then gradually beat them into the cheese mixture. Set aside.

Preheat the oven to 190°C (375°F) Gas 5. Roll out the pastry thinly on a floured surface and use to line the tart tin/pan. Prick the base all over with a fork, then chill or freeze for 15 minutes to set the pastry. Line with foil and baking beans, set on a baking sheet and bake blind in the centre of the preheated oven for 10–12 minutes. Remove the foil and beans, brush with the beaten egg yolk and cook for a further 5 minutes until golden.

Remove the pastry case from the oven, let it cool slightly, then pour the filling into the case and bake at the same temperature for 25–30 minutes, until risen and brown.

Remove from the oven and let cool in the tin/pan for 10 minutes, then transfer to a wire rack to cool completely. Arrange the figs, cut side up, on top of the tart. Warm the jelly and lightly brush the figs with it.

Protect the pastry edges with kitchen foil to prevent over-browning. Preheat the grill/broiler and set the tart close to the heat. Grill/broil quickly until the figs are just browning, then serve immediately.

Tiramisù with raspberries Tiramisù con lampone

This amazingly popular dessert is said to have originated in Venice in the 1950s, and is one dessert that actually benefits from being made the day before. For added texture, I like to grind real chocolate in a blender for layering and sprinkling. Some recipes are too sweet for my taste, but you can add more sugar to the cream mixture if you like. Make this in a large glass dish or in individual glasses for a special occasion.

150 g/5½ oz. dark chocolate (with over 60% cocoa solids)

300 ml/1¼ cups double/heavy cream

100 ml/½ cup freshly made Italian espresso coffee

6 tablespoons Marsala

250 g/9 oz. mascarpone

70 g/5 tablespoons caster/superfine sugar

2 tablespoons dark rum

2 egg yolks

24 sponge fingers/lady fingers (Italian *savoiardi* cookies)

200 g/7 oz. fresh raspberries, plus extra to decorate

a large serving dish or 4 glasses

Serves 4 generously

Put the chocolate in a blender or food processor and grind to a powder. Set aside. Pour the cream into a bowl and whisk until soft peaks form. Set aside.

Pour the espresso into a separate bowl and stir in 2 tablespoons of the Marsala. Set aside. Put the mascarpone in a third bowl and whisk in 3 tablespoons of the sugar, then beat in 2 tablespoons of the Marsala and the rum. Set aside.

To make the zabaglione mixture, put the egg yolks, 2 remaining tablespoons Marsala and the remaining 2 tablespoons sugar in a medium heatproof bowl and beat with a hand-held electric mixer or balloon whisk until well blended. Set over a saucepan of gently simmering water – the bottom should at no time be in contact with the water, and don't let the water boil. Whisk the mixture until it is glossy, pale, light and fluffy and holds a trail when dropped from the whisk. This should take about 5 minutes. Remove from the heat and whisk until cold. Fold in the whipped cream, then fold in the mascarpone mixture.

Dip the savoiardi, one at a time, into the espresso mixture. Do not leave them in for too long or they will disintegrate. Start assembling the tiramisù by arranging half the dipped savoiardi in the bottom of a serving dish or 4 glasses. Trickle over some of the leftover espresso. Add a layer of raspberries.

Sprinkle with one-third of the ground chocolate, then add half the mascarpone mixture. Arrange the remaining savoiardi on top, moisten with any remaining espresso, add some more raspberries and sprinkle with half the remaining chocolate. Finally spoon over the remaining mascarpone mixture and finish with a thick layer of chocolate and raspberries. Chill in the refrigerator for at least 3 hours (overnight is better). Serve chilled.

Zuppa inglese

This is the Italian version of English trifle and is found in many different variations, often containing chopped candied fruit. In the south of Italy, it is topped with meringue and becomes almost a French îles flottante with sponge. In Tuscany, it is served very liquid and soupy. My version has the meringue topping that I find makes the whole thing lighter. The traditional liqueur to use is a shocking pink, so you can add a little pink food colouring to any liqueur you are using to obtain the same effect.

300 g/10 oz. plain sponge cake, such as Madeira cake (*pan di Spagna*)

200 ml/¾ cup light rum

125 ml/½ cup Alchermes (pink Italian liqueur), Rosolio, Aurum or any orange-flavoured liqueur such as Cointreau

a few drops of pink food colouring (optional)

Vanilla custard

800 ml/3¼ cups full cream milk

1 vanilla bean, split lengthwise

8 eggs, separated (4 whites reserved)

120 g/½ cup caster/superfine sugar, plus extra for sprinkling

2 tablespoons plain/all-purpose white flour

a deep, heatproof ceramic or glass serving dish

Serves 6

Slice the cake thinly, cutting off any brown edges. Mix the rum and liqueur in a measuring jug/pitcher and add a few drops of food colouring, if using. Line the base of the serving dish with one-third of the sliced cake. Sprinkle the cake with 125 ml/½ cup of the rum mixture. Make the custard now, because it has to be warm when layering so it can soak into the cake.

Put the milk and vanilla bean in a saucepan and heat to just under boiling point. Put the egg yolks and 5 tablespoons of the sugar in a bowl and beat until pale and fluffy. Beat in the flour. Gradually whisk in the hot milk. Return the saucepan to the stovetop and cook over low heat, stirring constantly with a wooden spoon for about 10 minutes, until thickened to a pourable sauce-like consistency. Remove the vanilla bean.

Pour one-third of the custard over the cake and let it soak in for 5 minutes. Repeat with the second third of cake and rum mixture, pouring in half the remaining sauce. Repeat once more using up all the cake, rum mixture and sauce. Let cool completely – the sauce will develop a skin, but don't worry. Chill in the refrigerator for 2–3 hours. To finish, whisk the 4 egg whites with the remaining sugar until thick and glossy and holding soft peaks. Spoon this carefully over the trifle in blobs, then join the blobs together and use the back of a spoon to make swirls in the meringue. Sprinkle with extra sugar and heat under a medium grill/broiler for 1 minute, until lightly coloured. Serve while the meringue is still warm.

Profiteroles with a surprise · Profiteroles con sorpresa

Gianduja or gianduia is a chocolate and hazelnut mixture, famously associated with Turin, and is often used to flavour ice cream. This version of ice cream is classed as a semifreddo, which means that it stays soft when frozen, because of the meringue base.

Gianduja semifreddo

125 g/1 cup blanched toasted hazelnuts

125 g/5 oz. dark chocolate (with at least 65% cocoa solids), broken up

600 ml/2½ cups double/heavy cream

2 eggs, separated

175 g/1¼ cup icing/confectioners' sugar

Choux pastry

80 g/6 tablespoons unsalted butter, cubed

100 g/⅔ cup plain/all-purpose white flour, sifted twice with a pinch of sea salt

2–3 eggs, beaten

Hot chocolate sauce

100 g/4 oz. dark/bittersweet chocolate

200 ml/generous ¾ cup double/heavy cream

45 g/3 tablespoons caster/superfine sugar

45 g/3 tablespoons unsalted butter

a freezer container, about 1.25-litre/5-cup capacity

2 baking sheets, lined with parchment paper

Serves 6

To make the semifreddo, grind the hazelnuts very finely. Put the chocolate in a heatproof bowl set over a saucepan of hot water and let melt.

Put the cream in a bowl and whisk until soft peaks form, then fold in the nuts. Put the egg yolks in a second bowl with 2 tablespoons of the sugar and whisk until pale and creamy. Put the egg whites in a clean, dry bowl and whisk until soft peaks form. Add the remaining sugar to the whites, spoonful by spoonful, whisking between each addition, until very thick.

Stir the chocolate into the egg yolk mixture. Fold in the cream, then the meringue mixture. Spoon into a freezer container. Freeze for 12 hours until firm. Put a lined baking sheet in the freezer. Take the ice cream out of the freezer and put it in the refrigerator for 10 minutes before scooping into small balls with an ice cream scoop and setting apart on the frozen baking sheet. Freeze until hard.

Preheat the oven to 200°C (400°F) Gas 6. To make the choux pastry for the profiteroles, put the butter and 200 ml/¾ cup cold water in a heavy saucepan and bring slowly to the boil, so that by the time the water boils, the butter is completely melted. As soon as it hits a rolling boil, add all the flour at once, remove the pan from the heat and beat well with a wooden spoon. It is ready when the mixture leaves the sides of the pan.

Let cool slightly, then beat in the eggs, a little at a time, until the mixture is very smooth and shiny. If the eggs are large, it may not be necessary to add all of them. The mixture should just flop off the spoon when you bang it on the side of the pan – it should not be runny. Set teaspoons of the mixture at least 6–7 cm/2½–3 inches apart on the other lined baking sheet and bake in the preheated oven for 20–30 minutes or until deep golden brown.

Remove from the oven and split each one almost in two. Return to the oven to dry out for about 5 minutes. Cool on a wire rack. To assemble, put an ice cream ball in each one, pushing the halves almost together. Store in a box in the freezer until needed. Pile into a dish and soften in the refrigerator for 10 minutes before serving.

To make the chocolate sauce, put the chocolate, cream, sugar and butter in a saucepan. Stir until melted and pour immediately over the profiteroles.

Fluffy ricotta fritters

Frittelle di ricotta

Fluffy little puffs like these fritters are very popular in Italy, and are found in many guises. There is usually one to suit each saint, for his or her particular Saint's Day. Deep-fried snacks like these are part of Italian life and are seen as a real festive treat.

250 g/1 cup ricotta

2 eggs, at room temperature

2 tablespoons sugar

1 teaspoon vanilla extract

125 g/1 cup plain/all-purpose flour

1 teaspoon baking powder

½ teaspoon sea salt

vegetable oil, for deep-frying

icing/confectioners' sugar,
    for dusting

an electric deep-fryer

a tray lined with paper towels

Serves 4—6

Press the ricotta through a food mill, potato ricer or sieve/strainer into a large bowl. Put the eggs, sugar and vanilla extract in a separate bowl and whisk until pale and light. Fold into the ricotta.

Sift the flour with the baking powder and salt into a bowl, then fold it into the ricotta and egg mixture.

Heat the vegetable oil in the deep-fryer to 190°C (375°F). Have a tray lined with paper towels and a slotted spoon at the ready.

Drop level tablespoons of the mixture into the hot oil in batches of 6. Fry for 2–3 minutes until puffed and deep brown all over (you may have to turn them in the oil). Drain and serve immediately, dusted with icing/confectioners' sugar.

Index

Photography credits

Martin Brigdale:
Front endpapers, pages 3, 6–7, 10, 15–20, 23, 28, 31–34, 37, 39, 43, 45, 46, 49–54, 56, 57, 59, 60, 64–69, 71, 79–82, 89, 91, 94 right, 95 right, 99, 101, 102, 105, 106, 110, 112, 114, 116, 119, 123, 125, 126 right, 127 right, 130, 138, 139, 141–147, 149–152, 155, 157

Peter Cassidy:
Back endpapers, pages 8–9, 11–13, 21, 24–25, 36, 40–41, 47, 55, 62–63, 72–74, 76–77, 85 right, 92–93, 94 left, 95 left, 96, 97, 100, 113, 115, 120-122, 126 left, 129 both, 133 all, 134-136

Pages 2, 26, 27, 35, 70, 103
Giorgio & Ilaria Miani's Podere Casellacce in Val d'Orcia, Tuscany. Available for weekly hire – contact giorgiomiani@tin.it, see also www.ilariamiani.it

Richard Jung:
Pages 78, 84, 85 left, 85 centre, 86–88, 90

Yuki Sugiura:
Page 30

Debi Treloar:
Page 156
Katrin Arens www.katrinarens.it www.katrinarens.it

Chris Tubbs:
Page 1
Casa Colonica in Tuscany, interior design by Isabelle de Borchgrave, architect Jean Philippe Gauvin. Créations Isabelle de Borchgrave sprl, Rue Lens 24, B–1050 Brussels
www.isabelledeborchgrave.com, jp.gauvin@bracqgauvin.com

Page 5
Giorgio & Ilaria Miani's Podere Casellacce in Val d'Orcia, Tuscany. Available for weekly hire – contact giorgiomiani@tin.it, see also www.ilariamiani.it

Page 38
Toia Saibene & Giuliana Magnifico's home in Lucignano, Tuscany

Pages 83, 98, 148
Vanni & Nicoletta Calamai's home near Siena

Page 104
Podere Sala, Lori De Mori's home in Tuscany restored by architect André Benaim (benaim@tin.it)

Page 124
Toia Saibene & Giuliana Magnifico's home in Lucignano, Tuscany

Pages 140, 153
A house in Tuscany planned and decorated by architect Piero Castellini (studiocastellini@libero.it)

Ian Wallace:
Pages 108–109

Simon Walton:
Page 127 left